kaukasis

kaukasis

a culinary journey through
Georgia, Azerbaijan & beyond

OLIA HERCULES

MITCHELL BEAZLEY

An Hachette UK Company
www.hachette.co.uk

First published in Great Britain in 2017 by
Mitchell Beazley, a division of
Octopus Publishing Group Ltd
Carmelite House, 50 Victoria Embankment
London EC4Y 0DZ
www.octopusbooks.co.uk

ISBN 978 1 78472 164 0

A CIP catalogue record for this book is available from the
British Library.

Printed and bound in China

10 9 8 7 6 5 4 3 2 1

Publishing Director Stephanie Jackson
Managing Editor Sybella Stephens
Copy Editor Jo Richardson
Art Director Juliette Norsworthy
Photographer Elena Heatherwick
Designer Miranda Harvey
Food Stylist Olia Hercules
Prop Stylist Tabitha Hawkins
Cover Illustrator Grace Helmer
Map Illustrator Cara O'Sullivan
Senior Production Manager Peter Hunt

To the people of the Caucasus –
the most charismatic people in the world

Contents

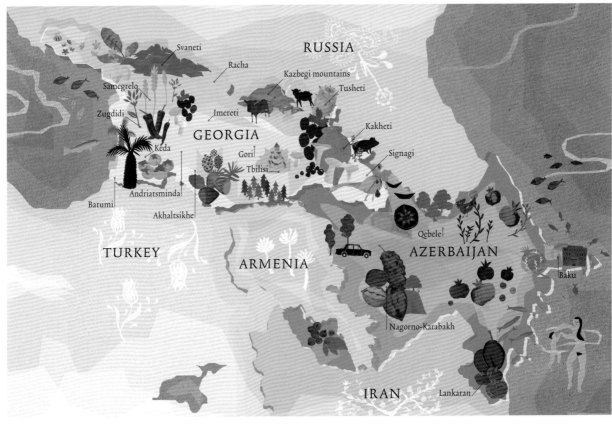

Introduction

Finding the name for this book was one of the hardest things I have ever had to do. How does one unite the idea of a childhood journey, memories and feelings of nostalgia with new-found knowledge of the Caucasus and its people? These folk may share the same geographical region, culture and much of their cooking, but they don't necessarily revere each other, or at least they often say they don't for various complicated reasons.

In the light of recent and not-so-recent events, where more and more neighbouring countries have gone to war and lost connections that have been cemented for centuries or have foolishly erected further barriers between them, I slipped into even more of a pitfall trying to navigate my way around and write sensitively about my family and friends' life-long experiences.

In times of great economic struggle, people fall apart. I have seen it happen on a personal level, where close friends, parents and their children or siblings break ties with each other because it is simply very hard. When it's hard to survive financially, hard to stay strong together and hard to make sense of history and events, it's easy to forget what unites us.

On a greater scale, the same happens with entire countries, which fall out and drag us even further along the road of alienation and conflict, inciting hatred, misunderstandings and worse. This happened to my Armenian family who are originally from Nagorno-Karabakh and have inspired me to write this book.

A war broke out in Karabakh in the 1980s, forcing them first to abandon their summer house and then to leave that region and eventually Azerbaijan's capital Baku to relocate to Kiev, the capital of Ukraine. Their house was largely destroyed, with only their huge beloved library room still standing with hundreds of books left abandoned and rotting on the shelves. Yet despite the anguish, mutual hostility and atrocities, I have not once heard my Armenian aunt say anything negative about Azerbaijanis. She has always reiterated that it was an artificially created conflict, like so many of them were at the time and still are.

I was taught from the start (perhaps in rather naive terms, but...) that people and human values are universal. Whether you are Armenian, Azerbaijáni or Georgian or one of any of the other Caucasian peoples, so much of the culture of the region is intertwined and destinies interwoven, and – on a more domestic level – so many cooking techniques and dishes are shared and borrowed. Geopolitics can often be an ugly, unfortunate reality, just like unemployment, financial difficulties and any of those other man-made afflictions. But I am glad that I grew up without having to take any sides. We cherished our Armenian, Azeri, Georgian, Ossetian, Karachai and Adegei friends all the same, equally interested in what they had to say, what they remembered, what they held dear and, of course, what they cooked!

Words kept running through my head: Caucasus, togetherness, communion, "as one", family, table, polyphony, layers, together. One word, I needed just one word to unite us all, but not in a tragic, forceful way like the word "Soviet" once did. I needed one word to unite our complicated histories, our families' memories, our new experiences in the most peaceful and natural way.

I tried a couple of options that I felt very strongly about, both powerful Georgian words, but sadly they didn't gel. In desperation, and following my best friend's wise council, I wrote a couple of pages of why I decided to write this book – a messy "stream of consciousness" kind of essay. And when I finished, I realized that I was overcomplicating things. The name doesn't have to be too clever, enigmatic or esoteric. The place itself, Caucasus, is mysterious enough.

Being an avid fan of etymology, I recalled reading that the name "Caucasus" possibly originated from the Scythian language (the Scythians being an ancient civilization from the Ukrainian steppe where I was born) and is akin to the gorgeous Greek word *Kaukasis*. It means "snowy mountain top", and at that moment the title of the book was born! At the very top of the Kazbegi mountains in northeastern Georgia, I saw a viewing platform with a massive mosaic. It was beautiful. What I loved the most was that the animals and people depicted have clearly defined outlines, but within their forms are made up of mismatched coloured tiles. This is how I feel about culture, and about traditions and recipes. The outlines are there, set in stone, but what's happening inside is a big puzzle of individual fragments, multicoloured and seemingly mismatched.

I hope you also approach this book as such. Get inspired by the outlines, but also feel compelled to create your own mosaic. This is my interpretation, a symbol, a vision of how to cherish tradition while also being open to creating something new.

Olia Hercules

"I like vegetables, especially in spring," declared our Georgian guide Shota. Such a simple thing to say, but it rang so true and got stuck in my head. It had so much meaning. In our modern world we can get tomatoes, cucumbers and herbs all year round. Of course, nowadays you can too in the Caucasus, but people still tend to eat seasonally. The first fresh vegetables of spring, the first herbs, the first sweet prickly cucumber – these ingredients are never better to enjoy than immediately after the long winter months.

roots, shoots, leaves & all

roots, shoots, leaves & all

Beetroot & plums

The combination of beets and plums was such a revelation to me that I immediately set about creating different versions of the authentic Georgian way of marinating beetroot in the tart plum sauce called *tkemali*. I couldn't choose which was the best, so I am giving two versions of the salad: the traditional approach and a roasted version for when plums are readily available but you can't be bothered to make the sauce. The roasted version will give you a taste similar to the original with the added pleasure of biting into caramelized plums and bitter leaves that contribute texture and a welcome savouriness. I use small tart Alycha plums here, but slightly underripe greengages or ordinary plums also work very well.

The original charkhali or plum-marinated beetroot

This is a method for making beetroot *charkhali* the authentic way, which is simple and delicious. But if you are short of time, you don't have to marinate it overnight – you can serve the *tkemali* immediately. It's brilliant, though, because if you have any left over, you can store it in the refrigerator and it will start to pickle. It should keep for up to a week if fully covered by the sauce. Serve with a slick of date molasses or honey if it seems too tart.

Serves 8 as a side

2 litres (3½ pints) water

2kg (4lb 8oz) beetroot, scrubbed really well

1 tablespoon sea salt flakes

500g (1lb 2oz) Tina's Fresh Tkemali, unsweetened (see page 23)

Bring the water to the boil in a saucepan, add the unpeeled beetroot and season with the salt. Cook for about 30–40 minutes until the beetroot is easily pierced with a knife but still *al dente*.

Drain the beets and leave until cool enough to handle, then peel and cut them into wedges.

Pop the beetroot into a bowl, pour over the *tkemali* and leave to marinate overnight in the refrigerator before serving.

VARIATION

Try roasting the same quantity of peeled beetroot wedges in a roasting tray in a preheated oven at 180°C (350°F), Gas Mark 4, for about 30–40 minutes until soft and starting to caramelize at the edges. Add the *tkemali*, covering the beets with it, and roast for a further 5–10 minutes. Then serve with a handful of chopped coriander and some thinly sliced spring onions.

Beets, plums & bitter leaves

Serves 4–6

2 tablespoons rapeseed or mild olive oil

500g (1lb 2oz) beetroot, peeled and quartered

5 plums, stoned and quartered

1 tablespoon red wine vinegar

150g (5½oz) Treviso (or ordinary) radicchio

1 red chilli, seeds in, sliced

2 teaspoons maple syrup or honey

2 garlic cloves, crushed

2 teaspoons sesame seeds, toasted

a handful of soft herbs – dill and coriander work really well here (optional)

sea salt flakes

Preheat the oven to 200°C (400°F), Gas Mark 6.

Add the oil to a roasting tray and heat it in the oven for 5 minutes.

Add the beetroot, plums and vinegar to the roasting tray, season with salt and roast for 30 minutes.

Leaving a little of the stalk in place, slice the radicchio into thin wedges. Add it to the beetroot tray with the chilli, maple syrup or honey and a bit more salt, and give it all a good stir. Roast for a further 10 minutes.

Add the garlic and stir it through the contents of the tray, then remove the tray from the oven.

Sprinkle over the sesame seeds and herbs (if using) and serve.

VARIATIONS
You can use any bitter crunchy vegetable instead of radicchio. Chicory would work well, as would sliced cultivated dandelion. Any toasted seed or nut can be substituted for sesame. I have also tried this with blackberries and blackcurrants instead of plums and it worked wonders – beetroot loves any dark, rich fruit that has a little acidity. I sometimes like to serve this with watercress or rocket.

Ia's salad

I love simple but unusual salads, when one tiny ingredient turns something so familiar into an incredible dish that you can't get enough of. This happened when I tasted Tomer Amedi's (Head Chef of The Palomar restaurant) mum's Yemeni tomato salad with green chillies and chopped lemon with its skin still on. And this happened again when I went to Megrelia (or Samegrelo, as Georgians call it) in western Georgia and met Ia, a school head teacher with a penchant for etymology, thin cigarettes and coffee. A modest addition of *adjika* makes this salad so piquant and moreish. I also love how the spring onions and herbs are cut into large chunks, almost treated like a vegetable rather than a mere seasoning.

Serves 2–4

1 head of Escarole or Romaine or similar lettuce, cut into large chunks

1 bunch of spring onions, sliced into 1cm (½-inch) chunks

¼ red onion, sliced (optional)

½ bunch of coriander, stalks and all, roughly chopped

½ bunch of flat leaf parsley, stalks and all, roughly chopped

½ cucumber, thinly sliced

2 ripe tomatoes, chopped (optional)

DRESSING

3 tablespoons white wine vinegar

1 teaspoon Red Adjika Salt (see page 62) or pinch of cayenne pepper

sea salt flakes, to taste (if using cayenne)

pinch of caster sugar or dash of honey (optional)

For the dressing, mix the vinegar and *adjika* salt or cayenne and salt together. Taste and add a little sugar if you think it needs it (I often do add sugar or honey here).

Mix the rest of the ingredients together in a large bowl, then pour over the dressing and gently combine with your fingers – Ia insisted I mixed it as if I was touching feathers.

Tips I would add the red onion if this salad is to be served with barbecued meats, otherwise leave it out for a much more delicate result. If you can't be bothered to make the adjika and can't find it ready-prepared, don't worry, this salad will be lovely with a simple lemon, salt and honey dressing spiked with some smoked paprika or a little cayenne.

roots, shoots, leaves & all

Satsebeli

Nobody makes small quantities of *satsebeli* in Samegrelo, western Georgia. They would normally use about 50kg (110lb) of tomatoes to bottle enough to last all winter. And no wonder, as this is an amazing sauce. It's good with roast chicken, it's incredible drizzled over eggs or polenta and it's also the bomb when drizzled inside a juicy lamb burger or served with refried *khinkali* dumplings (see page 85). The original recipe would have required you to buy a special oar and cistern for stirring and cooking this sauce, but I have scaled down the quantities for non-Georgian home use.

Makes approx. 500ml (18fl oz)

1.25kg (2lb 12oz) tomatoes, chopped

250g (9oz) red peppers, cored, deseeded and chopped

25g (1oz) garlic cloves, chopped

50g (1¾oz) Red Adjika Salt (see page 62) or 20g sea salt with a good pinch of cayenne pepper

sea salt flakes, to taste

sunflower oil, to cover (if storing)

If storing longer term, you will also need enough sterilized airtight bottles or jars to hold 2 litres (3½ pints) in total

Put the chopped tomatoes in a bowl with a handful of sea salt flakes, cover and leave overnight to release their juices if you have time. If not, blitz them in a blender or food processor.

Transfer the tomatoes to a saucepan, add the red peppers and cook slowly over a low heat for 40 minutes–1 hour until the peppers are soft and the tomatoes have reduced to a third of their original volume. Leave to cool a little, then blitz in the blender or food processor and pass through a sieve.

Put the mixture back into the cleaned pan, add the garlic and *adjika* and cook for a further 30 minutes, stirring from time to time to mix in the *adjika* and avoid a crust forming on top. Taste, and if needed season with salt – this sauce should be ever so slightly saltier than you think it needs to be if you want it to keep for a long time. But if you are planning to eat it within a week, season with as much salt as you feel comfortable with, then leave to cool and store in an airtight container in the refrigerator.

If storing over the winter, transfer the cooled sauce to sterilized airtight bottles or jars and pour a thin film of oil on top to help it keep for longer. Seal and store in a cool, dark place.

Kohlrabi, sorrel, radish & chicory salad with tkemali dressing

I love taking inspiration from ingredients that I encounter on my travels and using them in ways that wouldn't necessarily be used in their home country. *Tkemali*, the ubiquitous Georgian plum, garlic and wild mint condiment, is traditionally eaten with everything – meat, fish, eggs – but apart from beetroot (see page 13), not so much with vegetables. Its qualities, however, are those of a really superior dressing – tart, a little spicy and garlicky plus a hint of sweetness – and it works so well with bitter crunchy vegetables. Do experiment with the ingredients here; I bet it would work equally well with some young sweet cabbage, robust lettuce or radicchio.

Serves 4

1 tablespoon pomegranate molasses

50g (1¾oz) Tina's Fresh Tkemali (see page 23)

honey, to taste, if needed

2 heads of chicory, sliced lengthways into 8 wedges

1 kohlrabi, peeled and thinly sliced

50g (1¾oz) radishes, thinly sliced

25g (1oz) sorrel leaves (or watercress)

sea salt flakes

For the dressing, mix the molasses through the *tkemali*, then taste, adding some salt or a little honey if you think it's too tart. It should really taste strong and pack a punch.

Toss the chicory, kohlrabi and radishes in a bowl, then arrange in a serving dish with the sorrel leaves (or watercress) and serve with the dressing drizzled over.

Tina's fresh tkemali

Tkemali is one of the cornerstones of Georgian cooking. There are as many variations as there are households. Normally the formula involves cooking the tiny Alycha or tkemali plums until they can be passed through a sieve, getting rid of the stones and skin and leaving you with the most wonderful plum pulp. Then it is cooked down with garlic and other flavourings like dill. Tina, a village doctor, farmer and the gentlest soul, who lives high up in the mountains of Svaneti in the northwest, makes this version where the plums are hardly cooked. She prefers it fresh, she says, and I love her style. This recipe is perfect for cooking with or for dressing beetroot (see page 13).

Makes 1.2 litres (2 pints) if not cooked down too much

- 1.5kg (3lb 5oz) yellow and red Alycha plums (or greengages or ordinary plums)
- ½ tablespoon ground ombalo (or dried mint)
- ½ tablespoon dill seeds (or ½ teaspoon fennel seeds)
- 1 teaspoon ground coriander
- 1 teaspoon ground blue fenugreek
- 5 garlic cloves, grated
- ½ teaspoon cayenne pepper
- sea salt flakes and freshly ground black pepper

You will also need 4 x 300ml (10fl oz/½-pint) sterilized preserving jars

Put your yellow and red plums (or whatever greengages/plums you have managed to procure) whole into a saucepan. Add a splash of water and let them come up to the boil. Cook for about 10 minutes until they become soft and separate easily from their stones.

Leave the plums until cool enough to handle, then remove the skins and stones. If a little bit of skin remains, it's not a big deal.

Mix the plum flesh with the rest of the ingredients, season to taste and cook for a further 2 minutes.

While the sauce is still hot, transfer it to the sterilized jars, seal the jars and immerse them in a deep saucepan of simmering water for a few minutes. Then seal and store in a cool, dark place all winter or, if eating straight away, keep in the refrigerator.

Tip Although I love this version, sometimes the sauce turns out just too astringent (which it's supposed to be authentically), so I add a large tablespoon of molasses sugar or black treacle and cook it down for a further 10 minutes rather than 2 minutes. This is a version that has more body to it and is a little deeper in flavour, more like chutney.

The best herb growers and vendors in Georgia's markets are Azerbaijani women.
Georgians lovingly call them badji (sister) in Azerbaijani.

Mint adjika

This is my favourite paste of all time. It is so easy to make, keeps for months and is incredibly versatile. A lot of women in western Georgia would have a jar of this in their refrigerator. They mix it through stretchy cheese when they make their national western Georgian dish called *elardji*, and it does indeed go so well with creamy fresh cheeses, such as in the Fruit, Mint Adjika & Dairy toast recipe on page 26. Brush a smidgen on to some sourdough toast topped with good mozzarella. Alternatively, stir it through boiled new potatoes.

Makes about 375ml (13fl oz)

125g (4½oz) spearmint (or ordinary mint), stalks and all

10 green chillies, half deseeded

5 garlic cloves

20g (¾oz) sea salt flakes

Blitz everything together in a powerful blender or food processor to a paste, or bash it lovingly using a pestle and mortar if you want to feel like an authentic Georgian *bebia* (Grandma).

This is a wet flavoured salt, so use sparingly. Store in the fridge for up to 1 month.

Green adjika

There are as many *adjika* recipes as there are *tkemali* (plum sauce) recipes, and every woman has her own. I love this one that I picked up in the city of Zugdidi in the western Georgian province of Samegrelo. Stir a little bit through plain cooked pulses or through yogurt. It is also excellent used as a base for a dressing for roast root vegetables or with added gherkins or capers over soft-boiled eggs.

Makes about 400ml (14fl oz)

2 celery sticks, roughly chopped

1 bunch of coriander, leaves, stalks and roots (if the roots are available, well washed)

1 bunch of flat leaf parsley, stalks and all

1 bunch of basil, stalks only

5 garlic cloves, roughly chopped

10 green chillies (leave the seeds in if you like it hotter)

20g (¾oz) sea salt flakes

Blitz everything together in a powerful blender or food processor. You will end up with a wet, green paste.

Store in the refrigerator for up to 1 month.

Fruit, mint adjika & dairy

Georgia is a country that manages to completely mess with your head. Had I not had my son, I probably would have moved there at the first opportunity. Truth be told, I actually considered moving even with my toddler son. But when I was back in London, the trance I was in lifted and I came to my senses. This didn't happen to Ének Peterson, a young American who decided to take a short trip around Georgia but stayed on and is now cooking tasty, creative dishes in Vino Underground, a natural wine bar in Tbilisi. This is my version of a bruschetta she served me. It is one of the best combinations around. Sweet fruit, tangy cheese, spicy and fresh mint paste – nothing short of genius. Any seasonal fruit will work, such as Sharon fruit, pears or apples in winter, or nectarines or apricots in the summer. My Italian friends now say it's their favourite "bruschetta". I hope they won't be alone. Eat as a casual snack or make loads of little ones and feed a party.

Serves 5 as a snack

   5 thin slices of sourdough bread
   1 tablespoon Mint Adjika (see page 25)
   50g (1¾oz) mild goats' cheese or labneh
   2 firm apricots, stoned and sliced, or 1 Sharon fruit, thinly sliced
   mint leaves, to garnish

Toast the bread, then brush with the mint *adjika* – be careful, as it's really salty and should be used sparingly, as a seasoning.

Top with the goats' cheese or labneh and your choice of fruit and sprinkle over some mint.

Homemade matsoni

To make this recipe (a type of yogurt made with the special Caspian bacteria), the like of which you've never tasted before, you first need a *matsoni* starter. When I was writing this book in Svaneti, northwest Georgia, my brain was so overtaken by it all that I had a dream that I was by the shore of the Caspian Sea scraping ancient fossils with a spoon, "collecting" this bacteria. Surreal romantic visions aside, you can find this online (see page 234). Or go to a Georgian restaurant and ask them for some *deda* or a little *matsoni* in a plastic bottle. I've known people who have made contact with Georgians in their area on Instagram – the community is so friendly and welcoming, I am sure someone will be willing to help you. Failing all else, contact me and I'll give you some. A handful is all you need to begin creating something incredibly wonderful, healthy and, most importantly to me, tasty. It has so many uses in this book, and I am sure you will find new creative uses for it, too.

Makes approx. 2.1 litres (3¾ pints)
  2.1 litres (3¾ pints) raw milk
  1 heaped tablespoon *matsoni* or raw milk yogurt
  (available from good farmers' markets)

  You will also need a warm blanket or large towel

Heat the milk in a saucepan until it just "bites" your finger. Whisk the *matsoni* through the milk and immediately remove from the heat. Cover the pan with a lid, then wrap the pan in a warm blanket or large towel. Place somewhere warm for 24 hours. Do not move or disturb the pan, just leave it to sit.

The next day, the mixture should look like a thick yogurt, but this will depend on how fatty the milk you used was. You may have to leave it for a few hours' longer.

In the Caucasus, some people make a fresh batch of the yogurt every day and it is best used within 24 hours or so, otherwise it will become too sour. But any leftovers can be stored in the coldest part of the refrigerator and will be pleasant to eat for up to 4 days. It can be kept for longer (2 weeks) but will turn sour and will only be good used as a starter. If the milk has turned "hoochie" and smells of alcohol it is best not used for anything.

Courgettes & garlic matsoni

This dish is simplicity itself. It used to be made with mayonnaise throughout the ex-Soviet Union, but thank goodness that's all over and we can now use traditional premium dairy. As with all simple recipes, this is particulary tasty if you can source great home-grown or good-quality courgettes and make your own *matsoni*. If your courgettes are not the greatest, try using a mixture of all the soft herbs you like best to give them a bit of a lift. But if you have amazing vegetables and your own homemade yogurt, use just a little dill and let them sing their sweet, gentle song. And I love borage for its subtle cucumber flavour overtones.

Serves 4 as a side

   2 large courgettes

   4 tablespoons vegetable oil

   100g (3½ oz) Homemade Matsoni (see page 29) or good-quality natural yogurt

   2 garlic cloves, crushed

   1 tablespoon of your favourite mixture of soft herbs, roughly chopped

   sea salt flakes

Slice the courgettes lengthways into 5mm (¼ inch) strips.

Heat the oil in a large frying pan and fry the courgette slices on each side until deep golden. Remove and drain them on kitchen paper.

Mix the *matsoni* or yogurt with the garlic and add some salt, then taste – it should be really well seasoned, so add more salt if necessary. Drizzle the mixture over the courgettes and sprinkle over the herbs.

VARIATION
Try lightly coating the courgettes in flour before frying – it will give them a bit more body. Buckwheat flour adds a nice nuttiness to the flavour.

Chestnut plov with pumpkin & walnut crust

I happened to meet a film crew of old recipe hunters in Azerbaijan, a group of five men who travelled all around the country seeking out forgotten recipes for their TV show. My brother and I got lucky and went along. We climbed through freezing mountain springs and off-roaded until we reached a village where the most gorgeous woman cooked us a *plov* and told us about her life. She also told me about this *plov* with its most unusual *gazmakh* or crust. You can serve this with meat, but to me the chestnuts and plump dried fruit do the job. Since dried fruit is one of the main ingredients, try to find good-quality fruits with no added sulphites.

Serves 6

350g (12oz) basmati rice

250g (9oz) Delicata pumpkin or other good winter squash, peeled, deseeded and grated

100g (3½oz) walnuts, ground into a paste with a powerful blender or with a pestle and mortar

150g (5½oz) Clarified Butter (see page 53)

pinch of saffron threads

small pinch of rock salt

200g (7oz) peeled chestnuts, roasted and roughly chopped, or vacuum-packed

60g (2¼oz) ready-to-eat dried apricots, sliced

60g (2¼oz) raisins

fine sea salt

First, wash the rice well in several changes of cold water to get rid of as much starch as possible. Then cook it in a large saucepan in plenty of well-salted boiling water for about 7 minutes until it is almost cooked. Drain it well and spread it on a tray to let off a bit of the steam.

Mix the grated pumpkin with the walnut paste and a pinch of fine sea salt, combining the ingredients thoroughly (the moisture from the pumpkin and the walnut oils should help it stick together). Taste and add more salt if you think you need it.

Heat 40g (1½oz) of the Clarified Butter in a 23cm (9 inch) diameter heavy-based saucepan, then spread the pumpkin and nut paste all over the base of the pan in a thin layer and cook over a medium heat for 1–2 minutes. Reduce the heat to the lowest-possible setting and add the rice, in batches, making sure that it falls in loosely – try not to pack it down. Cover the pan with a tea towel and then cover with a lid and cook for 30 minutes.

Meanwhile, melt 70g (2½oz) of the Clarified Butter in a pan. Using a pestle and mortar, grind the saffron with the rock salt, then scrape it into the melted butter. Set aside to infuse.

Salim and Halima Akhmadov (centre), surrounded
by three generations of their family.

Once the rice has been cooking for 30 minutes, lift the lid and tea towel, then make holes in the rice with a handle of a wooden spoon and pour the saffron butter all over. Remove from the heat and leave, covered, while you prepare the nuts and dried fruit.

Heat the remaining Clarified Butter in a large frying pan and cook the chestnuts, dried fruit and a sprinkling of salt over a low heat for about 5–7 minutes until they look plump and are warmed through.

When the rice is *dan dan*, the Azerbaijani term for fluffy, perky, perfectly cooked rice, take it out of the pan gently and put into a beautiful serving dish. Now check your pumpkin crust – it should be nicely caramelized, not burnt, and if that's the case, gently scrape it off the base of the pan and sprinkle over the rice. Add the buttery chestnuts and dried fruit on top and serve alongside some sharp salads, whole bunches of herbs and grilled meat or vegetables.

Ekala pkhali

Ekala is a wild plant found in Georgia that resembles young vine shoots and has a mildly sour and pleasantly musky flavour. I love finding an ingredient as exotic as this at a market – it fills me with awe and a sense of wonder. Can you imagine seeing wild foraged food on sale at your local market like it was the norm?! I doubt you will be able to find ekala outside Georgia, but the walnut paste works perfectly well with any one of the other blanched leaves suggested.

Serves 2

300g (10½oz) ekala or purslane, Swiss chard, beetroot tops or spinach

2 small garlic cloves, peeled

¼ teaspoon cayenne pepper

½ teaspoon dried blue fenugreek

150g (5½oz) walnuts

2 tablespoons white wine vinegar or lemon juice

1 teaspoon honey, or to taste

sea salt flakes

Bring a saucepan of salted water to the boil and dip in your greens of choice to blanch – ekala and purslane need 30 seconds before immediately draining and refreshing under cold running water, Swiss chard stalks 2 minutes, Swiss chard leaves and beetroot tops a minute and with spinach I would just dip it in and out of the boiling water. As soon as the greens have cooled down in the cold water, drain them well.

To make the *pkhali* paste, bash the garlic cloves with some sea salt flakes in a mortar with a pestle. Then add the spices and the nuts, and keep grinding until the mixture starts to resemble a paste. Add the vinegar or lemon juice and honey to the paste and taste it, adding a little more salt or sweetness to your taste.

Toss the drained greens in the walnut paste and serve with bread for a light lunch or as part of a bigger feast.

VARIATION
Georgians also slightly overcook runner beans and then muddle them with the pestle alongside the paste in the mortar. In the West, we have been taught that overcooking beans is a mistake, and it usually is, but in combination with this fragrant paste, the "overcooked" runner beans provide flavour and comfort. Try it.

Badrijani nigvzit or aubergine rolls

There are are so many recipes for stuffed aubergines in the Caucasus – some simple, some more complicated. I tasted this in my beloved city of Zugdidi (western Georgia) and this is just how I have been taught to make it. It is one of those perfect universal recipes that will shine all over the world and is now my number one choice if I ever have to cater for a vegetarian friend. It is as filling as it is delectable.

Serves 4

6 tablespoons sunflower oil

2 large aubergines, halved lengthways

2 onions, diced

100g (3½oz) walnuts

1 garlic clove, crushed

1 small bunch of flat leaf parsley, leaves picked and finely chopped

1 small bunch of coriander, stalks and all, finely chopped

½ teaspoon Red Adjika Salt (see page 62) or some cayenne pepper

½ teaspoon Green Adjika (see page 25) (optional)

seeds of 1 small pomegranate

sea salt flakes, if needed

Heat 4 tablespoons of the oil in a large frying pan or griddle pan, add the aubergine halves cut side down and allow to colour. Flip them, then reduce the heat and cover the pan with a lid. The aubergine slices need to be cooked through, soft and malleable, so it may take up to 20 minutes for this to happen – be patient. If you prefer, brush the aubergine halves with the oil, sit them cut side up on a baking tray and roast in a preheated oven at 200°C (400°F), Gas Mark 6, for 15–20 minutes until nice and golden, then flip and cook for a further 15 minutes until the aubergines seem soft enough to be folded in two.

While the aubergines are cooking, make the stuffing. Fry the onions in the remaining 2 tablespoons of oil until golden, then leave to cool and strain off any excess oil.

Meanwhile, blitz the walnuts until really finely ground in an electric spice or coffee grinder.

Mix together the ground walnuts, cooled strained onions, garlic, herbs and both *adjikas*, if using, or cayenne really well. Taste and add salt if needed, then gently stir through half the pomegranate seeds.

Drain the aubergine halves on kitchen paper. Spread a tablespoon of the stuffing along each aubergine half, then fold in two. Place a tiny bit of the stuffing on top and add a few more pomegranate seeds to garnish.

Gia's mushrooms & egg

It was in the town of Signagi in the eastern Georgian region of Kakheti where I tried some of the most delicious and inventive, without being contrived, cooking. "Good food doesn't have to be complicated, overworked," remarked Gia, Head Chef at an incredibly beautiful restaurant (of natural wine fame – see page 233) called Pheasant's Tears. And I agree with him wholeheartedly. With a few wonderful ingredients, knowledge of tradition and a creative mind like Gia's, Georgian cooking is taken to another level. This dish was so simple, but I would award it and the others that we tasted numerous stars and accolades. Just find excellent mushrooms, really good eggs, some aromatics and a tiny bit of spice, and you have a beauty of a dish.

Serves 2 as a sharing starter

50g (1¾oz) unsalted butter

1 tablespoon olive oil

2 garlic cloves, sliced

2 field mushrooms, brushed clean

200g (7oz) field mushrooms or wild mushrooms, such as trompettes or chanterelles, brushed clean

1 egg

1 green chilli, thinly sliced (keep the seeds if you like heat)

a few sprigs of rosemary in winter or tarragon in summer

sea salt flakes and freshly ground black pepper

Preheat the oven to 180°C (350°F), Gas Mark 4.

Heat the butter and oil in an ovenproof dish in the oven, or in an ovenproof frying pan on the hob. Add the garlic and let it sizzle for a moment, just enough to release its aroma, then add all the mushrooms and spoon over the sizzling fat to cover them. Cook in the oven for 10 minutes, or cook on the hob over a medium-low heat, shaking from time to time, for about 5 minutes until the mushrooms have softened.

Crack the egg into the middle of the dish or pan and sprinkle over the chilli, herbs and some salt and pepper. Cook in the oven for 5–10 minutes until the whites are set and the yolk is cooked to your liking.

Adjapsandali

"How's life?" "Akh, my life is a total *adjapsandali* at the moment." This is what you may hear a couple of Georgians saying to each other, and it would mean that someone's life is in complete (but delicious) chaos. Here the term is applied to a ratatouille-style assortment of veg, to which you may respond, another ratatouille? But what a version it is. If ratatouille is a humble peasant, then *adjapsandali* is the knight of spring vegetable stews. There is nothing prosaic about this dish. If you are short of time or endearingly lazy, or have home-grown vegetables that are so flavoursome that they don't need any help with taste, skip browning the veg in the pan. Just layer them with the onion and cook in the oven, adding the herb paste and marigold powder or saffron at the very end. Whatever you do, don't skip the last step where you smash a variety of soft herbs with garlic – do it. This is what gives this seemingly modest dish its *cojones*. Saffron is not authentic – Georgians would add what they call Imereti saffron or yellow flower, i.e. marigold flowers dried and ground, and if you can find the good stuff, get it, as it tastes like floral fungi. But if marigold is not available, a tiny bit of saffron adds a certain *je ne sais quoi*.

Serves 4–6

4 tablespoons sunflower oil

2 potatoes, peeled and thinly sliced

1 aubergine, sliced into rounds

1 red pepper, cored, deseeded and chopped

1 green pepper, cored, deseeded and chopped

10 runner beans, chopped

1 large onion, thinly sliced

3 garlic cloves, 2 roughly chopped, 1 left whole

1 red chilli, (deseeded if you want less heat) chopped

pinch of powdered dried marigold petals (or a tiny pinch of saffron threads) (optional)

1 teaspoon dried blue fenugreek (or use ground coriander or ground cumin)

1 bunch of coriander, leaves, stalks and roots (if the latter are available, well washed)

1 large ripe tomato

handful of roughly chopped purple or green basil

handful of roughly chopped dill

handful of chopped tarragon

small handful of chopped summer savory (if available) or a pinch of dried

sea salt flakes and freshly ground black pepper

warm crusty bread, to serve

continued »

Heat 2 tablespoons of the sunflower oil in a large saucepan and (if you have the time and are after deep flavours) sauté the potatoes, aubergine, peppers and beans in batches briskly, adding a little bit more oil as you go if the pan becomes dry. Remove the vegetables to a bowl.

Now heat another tablespoon of oil in the pan, add the onion, the 2 chopped garlic cloves and chilli and cook slowly for about 15 minutes, drawing out the onion's sugars, until it is all meltingly sweet and golden. If you prefer a fresher flavour, skip this step and simply add the onion, garlic and chilli as they are to the rest of the veg.

Bash the marigold petals (or saffron) with some salt using a pestle and mortar and add a splash of water. Then add this together with the blue fenugreek (or other warm spices of your choice) to the pan.

Chop the coriander stalks and roots very finely and layer with the vegetables in the pan.

Cut the tomato in half and grate it. If it's a good tomato, I don't throw away the skin but chop it and use it, too. Add to the vegetables, season well with salt and pepper and add a splash of water if you think it needs it. Cover with a lid and cook gently for 30 minutes, then uncover and cook over a medium heat for a further 5 minutes.

Add the remaining garlic clove to your mortar with a little salt, the coriander leaves and all the other herbs, and gently grind with the pestle. Just before serving, stir this head-spinning herb paste through the warm vegetables and serve with a huge hunk of warm crusty bread.

Tip Don't stress about what soft herbs you can find – this is not a rigid formula. Use whatever soft, fresh aromatics you can procure including basil, coriander, tarragon, dill, chervil and marjoram, but keep away from sage. Mix and match them together with some salt and garlic, and you will transform a simple ratatouille into the delicious chaos that is our lives and... adjapsandali!

Cauliflower steak gratin

Aunt Nina really loves her cauliflower, and she is not shy to get creative with it. She actually uses processed "burger" cheese here and I still enjoy the dish (this may be the only "guilty" pleasure I will ever have), but I think using a good-quality melty cheese is preferable.

Serves 4 as a side
   1 head of cauliflower
   10g (¼oz) unsalted butter
   1 tablespoon vegetable oil, plus extra if using the onion
   1 onion, thinly sliced (optional)
   4 eggs, lightly beaten
   2 small garlic cloves, finely grated
   150g (5½oz) raclette or Ogleshield cheese, grated
   1 tablespoon chopped coriander
   1 tablespoon chopped dill
   sea salt flakes and freshly ground black pepper

Preheat the oven to 180°C (350°F), Gas Mark 4.

Slice the cauliflower, including the stalks and leaves (if they aren't too manky), into steaks 3cm (1¼ inches) thick. Some florets will break away, but keep those as well.

Heat the butter and oil in a large frying pan, and when really hot, brown the cauliflower steaks on each side. Transfer to a gratin dish.

If using the onion, add some more oil to the frying pan, add the onion slices and cook gently until soft and golden. This will take 10 minutes or a bit longer, so if you can't be bothered, leave this step out.

Mix the eggs, garlic, cooked onion, if using, and cheese together, and season with salt and pepper. Pour over the cauliflower and bake for 15–20 minutes until the eggs are set and golden. Scatter with the chopped herbs before serving with a fresh green salad.

Gia's polyphony courgettes

I would never in a million years think to pair courgettes and berries, but the dish that Gia made for us at his restaurant Pheasant's Tears in Signagi, in the eastern region of Kakheti, was one of the best I have ever eaten. Just like a Georgian polyphonic song that may sound like dissonance to those who are used to the jolly simplicity of pop songs, it was as multilayered as the colours and flavours of a Georgian landscape. All the ingredients were outstanding and sang their own notes, but also came together to create a unique whole.

Serves 4 as a side
- 4 tablespoons sunflower oil
- 4 shallots or small onions, halved
- 2 courgettes, cut into 2cm (¾-inch) rounds
- 5 garlic cloves, cut in half vertically
- 2 long green chillies, bruised but left whole
- handful of fresh sour cherries and/or redcurrants
- sea salt flakes and freshly ground black pepper

Heat the oil in a large frying pan, add the shallots or onions and cook over a medium-low heat until they soften and start turning golden. Remove from the pan.

Add the courgette rounds and brown on each side.

Reduce the heat, add the garlic and chillies and season everything really well. Cook for 3 minutes.

At the very end, add the sour cherries and/or redcurrants and switch off the heat. Taste again and season with some extra salt and pepper if it needs it. Serve with sourdough bread or as part of a bigger feast.

Nutty tomato & cucumber salad

Tomatoes and cucumber are another of those standard combinations, but add some nuts, chillies and an interesting mix of herbs and you have a different beast altogether. Traditionally, Georgians would of course use walnuts, but do experiment with your favourite nut. I love adding pistachios to this, and my favourite crazy combination of herbs.

Serves 2

- 2 teaspoons clear honey
- 2 tablespoons white wine vinegar or sherry vinegar
- 1 green chilli, diced
- 3 good-quality tomatoes, sliced or chopped
- 1 cucumber, sliced
- 2 spring onions, sliced
- 1 garlic clove, grated
- handful of chopped purple or green basil
- handful of chopped coriander
- handful of chopped dill
- 50g (1¾oz) pistachio nuts or walnuts, toasted and chopped

For the dressing, mix the honey into the vinegar, add the chilli and leave for about 15 minutes to infuse.

Mix the salad vegetables, garlic and herbs together in a bowl, then dress with the dressing, sprinkle over the pistachios or walnuts, and wow!

Tomato & raspberry salad

This salad came about when Ének, a first-generation Hungarian who had settled in Georgia, picked out some extremely good tomatoes at a market in Tbilisi. Inspired by Hungarian-rooted chefs from Bar Tartine in San Francisco who do a version of this salad with sour cherries, she made one with raspberries, toasty unrefined sunflower oil and some green coriander seeds and flower heads. I know tomatoes and raspberries sound like a combination that should just be left alone, but it actually really works if you use excellent tomatoes, although not with hard, flavourless supermarket tomatoes. The tomatoes need to be ripe, sweet, flavoursome and juicy fruit so that they almost equal the raspberries in texture and juiciness. Strong, savoury, soft herbs also go very well here. Try marjoram or oregano mixed with mint or coriander leaves, dill or tarragon – you are going for intensity here. And make sure you season it really well with good flaky sea salt.

Serves 4 as a side

4 large super-ripe tomatoes

10 firm yellow, green and red cherry tomatoes

8 raspberries

5 black olives, pitted and torn

3 tablespoons unrefined sunflower oil

a few coriander flower heads or 3 sprigs of marjoram, leaves picked

1 sprig of mint, leaves picked and large ones torn

4 sprigs of dill, chopped

¼ mild onion, thinly sliced

sea salt flakes and freshly ground black pepper

Cut the tomatoes into sections. Your tomatoes should be so ripe that you will end up with loads of juice on your chopping board. Don't throw it away but add it to a bowl to use as part of the dressing.

Pop the tomatoes on to a serving plate and scatter over the raspberries and olives.

Whisk the unrefined sunflower oil into the reserved tomato juices and pour over the salad. Season generously with some salt and pepper, and sprinkle over the herbs and onion. The juices remaining at the bottom of the salad are made for bread-mopping.

Tip *If you can't find the correct sunflower oil, try another nutty oil. Mix a little sesame oil with some avocado or rapeseed oil, or try walnut oil if you can find the good stuff.*

Serdakh or aubergines & tomatoes

We sampled this simple yet satisfying, silky vegetarian dish in Lankaran in the southeastern region of Azerbaijan. There are many excellent aubergine and tomato dishes to be found all over the world, but this one slipped down so amazingly well and we just couldn't figure out what it was that made it extra moreish. I've never cooked aubergines in butter before, so it was a revelation to discover that clarified butter was the key, along with a copious amount of roughly chopped and caramelized garlic. Of course you can use oil instead, but – trust me – clarified butter makes the dish taste so unusual but strangely not heavy or buttery in a French way. Make a big pot and eat it hot or warm with a hunk of lovely bread and bunches of herbs.

Serves 2 as a main or 4 as a side

- 8–10 baby aubergines or 3 large
- 100g (3½oz) Clarified Butter (see page 53)
- 10 garlic cloves, roughly chopped
- 6 flavoursome tomatoes, halved across the equator, or some small, colourful tomatoes, left whole, or a mixture of both
- 200ml (7fl oz) water, vegetable or chicken stock
- pinch of caster sugar, if needed
- sea salt flakes and freshly ground black pepper

TO SERVE
- lavash flatbreads or any other flatbread, torn
- 1 small bunch of each or any of the following: dill, coriander, basil

If you are using baby aubergines, make 2 incisions in the shape of a cross in their rounded end as if you were going to quarter them lengthways, but don't cut into them further. I leave the stalks intact, as they look so pretty. If using large aubergines, trim and slice them about 15mm (⅝ inch) thick.

Heat 2 tablespoons of the Clarified Butter in a heavy-based flameproof casserole dish over a medium heat and fry the garlic while you keep stirring it. You want it to turn deep golden and stay juicy, but not become dry or burnt. Tilt the pan so that the butter and garlic collect in one corner – this way you will confit it. It will take about 2–5 minutes. The smell will be incredible as the garlic loses its harshness and becomes soft, sweet and gently caramelized. Take the garlic out and set aside. Do not wipe out the pan unless it looks burnt.

Heat another 2 tablespoons of the Clarified Butter in the same pan over a medium-high heat and fry the aubergines until they are well browned all over. Be patient and the skin will blister and the white flesh will soften, but it may take about 10 minutes – they really need to start collapsing. Take them out and set aside; you can leave them to drain over kitchen paper if you like. Again, do not clean the pan.

continued »

Heat another 2 tablespoons of the Clarified Butter in the same pan, add the tomatoes, cut side down, and cook them just on that side over a high heat until they catch some colour and the skins look wrinkled. If the tomatoes are ripe, use a pair of tongs to lift the skins off the tomatoes and discard. If they aren't, you may need to flip them, cook on the skin side briefly and then take the skins off. Sometimes I'm too lazy to take the skins off at all.

Now return the aubergines and garlic to the pan and add the liquid. Do try using chicken stock if you are not vegetarian, as it adds an extra layer of flavour. Water is absolutely fine, though, if you want the dish to remain as hassle free as possible. Season with salt and pepper (but go easy on the salt if you salted the aubergines previously) and add a pinch of sugar if your tomatoes are not the sweetest. Cook over a medium heat for about 15 minutes until the liquid has reduced by half and the aubergines are properly cooked through.

Serve with pieces of torn lavash or any other flatbread, or regular bread, and some sprigs of fresh herbs. This is also really lovely eaten with simply cooked rice or sliced tomatoes and cucumbers.

Clarified butter

In India, the ancient holistic healing system of Ayurveda prescribes a shot of ghee, aka clarified butter, as a detox agent for purifying the body, while in Azerbaijan, they love it so much that they serve their *plov* with extra for pouring over. The impoverished Molla Nasreddin, a satirical fictional character from Azerbaijani classical literature famous for mocking rich folk, and his wife were hungry one evening, so the story goes, when he asked, "To make a good *plov*, wife, what do you need?". The wife retorted, "We don't have even enough money for bread!" To which he replied, "Why don't we just dream about it... what would we need?" "1kg of rice, 1kg of ghee and 1kg of meat," his wife said. "Darling, what are you talking about," he exclaimed, "1kg of ghee to 1kg of rice – that is outrageous!" "Yes," she countered, "We are poor in reality, so just let me dream of that lovely fatty, buttery *plov*."

When you encounter *plov* recipes in this book, the quantities for clarified butter are very close to this. You can use less, but if like Molla's wife, like me, don't dream: go for it!

Makes approx. 900g (2lb)
  1.5kg (3lb 5oz) unsalted butter

Preheat the oven to 100°C (212°F/lowest possible Gas mark).

Put the butter into a pan and leave in the oven, uncovered, for the whole day. Every 2 hours, skim off the foam from the surface of the butter and discard, then pour off some of the clear liquid from the top into a container, making sure that the milk solids remain in the base of the pan.

Store the clarified butter in an airtight container in the refrigerator, where it will keep for up to about 2 weeks.

Alternatively, you can use this quick method, as we did when I worked in restaurants, but there is a greater risk of the milk solids sticking to the base of the pan:

Put the butter into a large saucepan over a low heat and simmer for about 30 minutes, skimming off the foam as it rises to the surface.

Pour off the clear liquid into a container, leaving the milk solids behind in the pan. Store as above.

Tip *The remaining butter solids (called ayran in Azerbaijan) are amazing mixed into a bread dough such as my Ossetian Pie Dough (see page 80).*

Purslane with tahini & garlic

Purslane grows in the wild all over Georgia, often spreading its delicate limbs along the soil between grape vines and even through asphalt. It is at its best in spring, but it can still be found and is often pickled in the autumn. Gia (Head Chef of the Pheasant's Tears restaurant in Signagi) cooked this so simply, but it was one of those dishes that I will never forget: still-crunchy purslane, a delicately balanced tahini dressing and a little bit of raw garlic crushed over the finished dish at the very end. Tahini is not typically Georgian – a walnut dressing would be more authentically regional (you can use *pkhali* instead; see page 35) – but even Georgians are starting to creatively fuse cuisines (thank you, Yotam), and it's not hard to get tahini in Georgia. That milky, foggy morning when we tried it along with some meaty wild oyster mushrooms, its delicate flavour worked ever so well.

Serves 2 as a side

2 tablespoons lemon juice

1 teaspoon good-quality honey

1 wet garlic clove or ½ ordinary garlic clove, finely grated

2 tablespoons tahini

350g (12oz) purslanc (or spinach)

sea salt flakes

For the dressing, mix the lemon juice with a good pinch of salt, then add the honey and garlic and stir to help it dissolve.

Gradually mix the lemon juice mixture into the tahini until the dressing becomes silky and pourable. Don't worry if the tahini stiffens at first – it will relax and loosen as you keep stirring and trickling in the liquid. But do add a splash of cold water if it remains stiff.

Put a saucepan of water on to boil. Drop the purslane into the water. Count to 30, drain, then cool under cold running water. Squeeze the water from the purslane, then pat it dry with kitchen paper.

Dress the greens with the tahini dressing and enjoy in the sun with crusty bread and some simple grilled meat or aubergines.

VARIATION

If you have the time, make some *satsivi* (see page 136) and use it in place of the tahini. Make sure that it's of pourable consistency by letting it down with some stock, lemon juice or water.

Cauliflower, brown butter & crumbs

Aunt Nina, an Armenian growing up in Azerbaijan, was a mechanical engineering student in the 1960s. Just before the exams, sat at her Azerbaijani friends' table with sheets of paper covered with lines and scribbles scattered around, they had a snack. No crisps in those days, but in my view they had something a lot better – cooked cauliflower florets, a dish with melted butter and blitzed *sukhariki* or dried breadcrumbs. The cauliflower was picked, dipped in the butter, then the breadcrumbs and devoured. Soft, buttery, crunchy – a student snack to inspire.

Serves 2 as a revision snack
- 1 tablespoon olive oil
- 1 head of cauliflower, about 550g (1lb 4oz), divided into florets
- 100g (3½oz) unsalted butter
- 50g (1¾oz) stale sourdough bread
- handful of finely chopped flat leaf parsley
- 1 red chilli, diced
- 1 teaspoon ground sumac (optional)

Preheat the oven to 200°C (400°F), Gas Mark 6. Brush a large baking tray with the olive oil, spread out the cauliflower florets and roast for about 30 minutes until they are cooked through and starting to colour at the edges.

Meanwhile, to make the brown butter, heat the butter in a frying pan and let it sizzle until it starts smelling sweet and nutty. Take the pan off the heat as soon as you smell it and it turns a deep golden colour, pour the contents into a cold bowl and set aside.

To make the sourdough crumbs, blitz the bread in a blender or food processor and, if necessary, spread out on a baking tray and place in the bottom of the oven for a few minutes to dry. Then mix with the parsley, chilli and sumac, if using.

Do your homework or exam revision/work and dip the cauliflower florets first into the brown butter, then into the sourdough crumbs. Or drizzle the butter over the cauliflower along with some cooked white beans and scatter over the crumbs to make a side dish for some grilled chicken or fish.

Tips *You can alternatively put the cauliflower in a roasting tray, dot loads of butter around it and add a little chicken stock. Roast for about 30 minutes, then for the last 5 minutes of the cooking time, add the breadcrumbs and sumac.*

Ramsons, unrefined sunflower oil & vinegar

If you ever come across ramsons or wild leeks or wild garlic, try eating the bulbs and leaves as simply as this. Do be sure to seek out the best unrefined sunflower oil you can. Failing that, any other flavoursome fresh nut oil would also do nicely. Earthy ramsons, sea salt, a little kick of acidity, raw thinly sliced onion and a slick of nut oil. Often the simplest things are the most satisfying. Serve as part of a bigger spread or as accompaniment to some grilled pork.

Serves 2 as a side

    300g (10½oz) ramson (wild leek or wild garlic) bulbs, well washed

    ½ small mild onion, thinly sliced

    2 tablespoons good-quality sherry vinegar

    sea salt flakes

    1 teaspoon granulated sugar (optional)

    2 tablespoons unrefined sunflower oil

Blanch the ramson bulbs in boiling water for about 1 minute, then drain and refresh under cold running water, or steam for about 2 minutes – they should soften but still have a bit of bite.

If your onion is strong, soak the slices in some iced water for a few minutes, then drain and dry well.

Toss the ramsons in the vinegar and sprinkle over the salt to taste. Leave them to pickle for 15 minutes if you have the time. I sometimes add a teaspoon of sugar at this stage, too, but it's not traditional.

Finally, scatter over the onion and drizzle over the nutty oil.

Red adjika salt

There are numerous types of *adjika*, ranging from dry garlic and chilli salt to chilli pastes. The commercially produced watery sauces are best avoided. My friend Ia called this recipe the *generalnaya adjika*, and it's the mother of all *adjikas*.

People rarely make this at home and I have been told that only professionals know the secret to the perfect general *adjika*. But I am never deterred in such situations, so I grabbed a 3kg (6lb 8oz) tub at the market in Zugdidi, and brought it back to London to begin my experiment. You will need to source some good blue fenugreek or what the Georgians call *utskhosuneli*, which is used in numerous dishes in this book. It is extremely versatile, so just apply your imagination and creative flair with abandon. If all fails, you will find details of an online supplier of the ready-made salt on page 234. Use it sprinkled over eggs or used in a salad dressing (see page 16).

Makes about 750g (1lb 10oz)
- 200g (7oz) ground blue fenugreek
- 100g (3½oz) ground coriander
- 65g (2¼oz) dried marigold petals or powder

- 40 garlic cloves, peeled
- 100g (3½oz) cayenne pepper (or the same quantity of fresh red chillies if you want to make a wet paste – see Tip below)
- 200g (7oz) sea salt flakes

Bash everything together using a pestle and mortar, or pass through a meat mincer, which is what's mostly used these days, as it results in neat red salt pellets that keep very well out of the refrigerator.

What you will end up with essentially is a flavoured salt, so use it sparingly. It will keep for a couple of months in an airtight container in a cool, dry place.

VARIATION
To make a wet paste version, Wet Red Adjika, simply use fresh red chillies instead of the cayenne. Store the paste in the refrigerator in a sterilized airtight jar, adding a thin film of oil on top if you want it to keep for longer.

Svaneti salt

Georgians love their slightly moist garlic- and chilli-flavoured salts, and *Svaneti* salt is justifiably famous in the country as it is such a delight – garlicky, herby and a little spicy. This is particularly good stirred into Homemade *Matsoni* (see page 29) or natural yogurt, or used as a seasoning for anything you like. Try it sprinkled on Fresh Homemade Cheese (see page 107) and ripe tomatoes or cucumbers.

Makes 550g (1lb 4oz)

300g (10½oz) sea salt flakes

1 tablespoon coriander seeds, ground into a powder

1 tablespoon ground blue fenugreek

1 teaspoon caraway seeds

1 teaspoon powdered dried marigold petals

1 tablespoon hot chilli flakes or hot paprika

50g (1¾oz) garlic, crushed

Mix the salt with all the dry spices, then add to a blender or food processor and blitz with the crushed garlic.

Transfer the salt to a large airtight container and store in a cool, dark place. This quantity should last you a couple of years but is best consumed within 6 months.

Tip *If sourcing these specific spices is too much of a chore, there are suppliers that sell ready-made Svaneti salt – see page 234 for details.*

Samegrelo roast pumpkin & red adjika

Sweet caramelized pumpkin or squash smothered in *adjika*, a spicy, salty chilli paste with blue fenugreek, was a revelation to me. Use the best-quality nuts you can find – walnuts are wonderful when in season.

Serves 4 as a side

    1 small pumpkin or butternut squash, unpeeled
    2 tablespoons rapeseed or olive oil
    2 tablespoons Wet Red Adjika (see page 62) or shop-bought
    handful of nuts, such as walnut, pecan nuts or hazelnuts, ground
    sea salt flakes

TO SERVE
    50g (1¾oz) Homemade Matsoni (see page 29) or natural yogurt
    let down with 1 tablespoon water
    handful of soft herbs, such as coriander, dill, basil, chervil and fennel tops

Preheat the oven to 200°C (400°F), Gas Mark 6.

Cut the pumpkin or squash in half lengthways and then cut into half moons 2cm (¾ inch) thick. Spread out over a baking tray, drizzle over the oil and season lightly with salt. Roast for 30–40 minutes until the pumpkin or squash starts catching at the edges.

Mix the *adjika* paste with the ground nuts, then spread it all over the pumpkin or squash. Reduce the oven to 160°C (325°F), Gas Mark 3, and roast for a further 10 minutes.

Serve drizzled with the *matsoni* or yogurt and your favourite herbs alongside some grilled meat and a fresh salad.

Tip If you can't be bothered to make adjika but haven't been able to source a decent version of the shop-bought stuff (not the watery tomato-based adjikas you can find in Russian shops), use a good-quality harissa. You can also make a warm salad with the pumpkin or squash – just add some bitter leaves or watercress.

Savoury peach & tarragon salad

We are used to tarragon in creamy sauces in the West but mainly just with chicken, and it remains such an underused herb, often declared as too strong and dominant. But Georgians love it and it finds its way into many, many dishes. We made this in Tbilisi in June, inspired by the gorgeous local produce. A savoury salad made only with fruit may seem unusual, but it works. Sour gooseberries or grapes combined with sweet peaches (or nectarines) along with savoury tarragon and salt makes a dream accompaniment to some grilled pork or lamb chops, or roasted meaty summer squashes.

Serves 2 as a side

  2 peaches, stoned and sliced

  50g (1¾oz) gooseberries or grapes (or 4 tart plums, stoned and sliced)

  ½ small bunch of tarragon, leaves picked (or a few fennel fronds)

  2 tablespoons lemon juice

  ¼ small red chilli, deseeded and diced

  ½ teaspoon caster sugar or honey

  1 small garlic clove, grated

  sea salt flakes and freshly ground black pepper

Arrange the peaches and gooseberries or grapes on a plate. Mix the tarragon leaves with the lemon juice, fresh chilli, sugar or honey, garlic, some salt and a generous pinch of pepper, then pour the dressing over the fruit and serve.

VARIATION

Mix a handful of pumpkin seeds with ½ tablespoon of maple syrup, a pinch of chilli flakes and some salt, spread them out on to a lined baking sheet and roast in the oven at 180°C (350°F), Gas Mark 4 for 5 minutes. Remove from the oven, leave to cool, then use as a savoury topping.

Turshulash-style roots & beans

I love when traditional recipes inspire or are given a slight makeover. Zulya was a piano teacher at a conservatory in Baku (which she still does part-time), but 16 years ago she became so obsessed with baking that she opened a small bakery in her garage. She decorated it with fabrics to make it look exotically (for Baku) European. They now have five beautiful pastry shops across Baku and are some of the loveliest people I've ever met. Zulya's mum comes from Lankaran in southeastern Azerbaijan close to the Iranian border and she often draws inspiration for her dishes from her mother's heritage. *Turshulash*, which literally translates as "sour dinner", is one such dish, a gorgeous seven-bean (or rather legume including chickpeas, green and red lentils, as well as corn), carrot and beetroot combo from Lankaran. She calls this salad "*turshulash z-style*", which annoys her husband Rufat (almost endearingly, as he is such a lovely guy), as he says it's a false representation and demands that she finds a new name for it. But I'm with Zulya – traditional-inspired dishes should hint at their origins.

Serves 6 as a side

500g (1lb 2oz) celeriac, peeled and cut into 2cm (¾ inch) dice

500g (1lb 2oz) candy or regular beetroots, peeled and and cut into 1cm (½ inch) dice

2 ripe tomatoes, grated

1kg (2lb 4oz) squash, peeled and cut into 2cm (¾ inch) dice

250g (9oz) quinces, peeled, cored and diced

2 tablespoons maple syrup or honey

3 tablespoons Alycha paste (*tursha*) or tamarind paste

400g (14oz) can red kidney beans, drained

sea salt flakes

Put the celeriac and beetroots into a saucepan, cover with cold water, then add some salt and the tomato pulp and bring to the boil. Reduce the heat and simmer for about 15 minutes or until the roots are tender.

Using a slotted spoon, remove the vegetables from the water in the saucepan and set aside. Add the squash and quince to the pan. Bring to the boil and then reduce the heat and simmer for about 15 minutes or until the squash is tender and quince is soft but still a little al dente.

Remove the squash and quince to the bowl with the other vegetables. Add the maple syrup to the vegetable cooking liquid and reduce over a high heat until only about 200ml (⅓ pint) is left in the pan. Remove from the heat, return the vegetables to the pan and stir them through, then leave to cool completely. You should end up with a kind of a salad with a loose dressing that tastes strongly of all the vegetables and has a sweet and sour note. Mix the beans through and serve as a side dish or mixed with some bitter leaves like a winter salad.

Herb kükü

"I tried an Azerbaijani herby omelette called kükü!" I announced excitedly. "That dish was originally Iranian!" was Sabrina Ghayour's response – there is no escaping her intensely Persian focus. While I agree with her that this dish definitely has Persian roots, it is also treasured in neighbouring Azerbaijan. I really love the name (it sounds so playful), love how herby it is (it's mostly herbs held together by a little egg) and love the sprinkling of sumac on top. You can fry it in oil if you wish, but I do love soft herbs cooked in butter – there is so much satisfaction to be had from a combination of fresh, fragrant flavour, creamy dairy and eggs. Play around with the combination of soft herbs; there are endless variants to enjoy – I often use watercress, spring onion, sorrel, spinach or wild garlic. Serve with flatbreads, a simple tomato salad (see page 47) and some natural yogurt with chopped cucumber, chilli, salt and a tiny bit of garlic.

Serves 4

150g mixture of soft herbs, such as coriander, dill, purple or green basil, tarragon and chives

4 eggs

1 garlic clove, finely grated

3 spring onions, finely chopped

20g (¾oz) Clarified Butter (see page 53) or ordinary butter and a drop of vegetable oil

½ teaspoon ground sumac

sea salt flakes

Remove any tough stalks from your mixture of herbs, then finely chop the softer stalks together with the leaves.

Whisk the eggs with some salt and the garlic, then stir in all the chopped herbs and spring onions.

Heat the Clarified Butter in a 23cm (9 inch) diameter frying pan and add the herby eggs. Cook, without touching it, over a medium-low heat for about 5 minutes until the eggs are just set and the underside develops a golden crust.

Now comes the tricky bit. To flip the kükü, cover the pan with a big plate, turn it upside-down on to the plate, then slide the kükü back into the pan. Continue cooking for 1 minute until the other side is golden, then remove from the heat and slide it on to a serving plate. Sprinkle the sumac on the top and serve.

VARIATION
You can also add a handful of lightly toasted and crushed walnuts to the kükü. For a winter version of the dish, use thinly sliced Swiss chard or beetroot tops or sweet white cabbage instead of the herbs.

I witnessed one of the most impressive examples of bread-making I have ever seen in my life in the tiny village of Andriatsminda. Galina, who is a prolific farmer and a perfect example of the Georgian *dedakatsi* (an impossibly strong, if self sacrificial, Georgian woman), had her own baking room – essentially a dark basement space with a wood-fired oven. Without wasting any of the heat that the oven provided, she baked four different types of bread, each taking its turn when the temperature of the oven was just right for it. First, when the oven was at its hottest, a type of flatbread went in, called *lavashi*. When that was cooked and fire had become a little less fierce, the second bread went in, one with a hole inside called *shoti*. After that, her incredible *khachapouri* were ready, and finally, when the oven began to cool down, she put in the largest bread, *somini*, which needs low and slow baking. The breads were then cooled on a rack made out of hazelnut branches. This ingenious way of economizing on energy, utilizing every bit of power that the burning wood can provide, is incredible.

flour & ash

Marina's kada lobiani

There are many ways to make *khachapuri*, but I loved the technique I saw in Akhaltsikhe in southern Georgia the most, where it was folded a few times with either butter or pork lard added between the folds, to create the most gorgeous, flaky flatbreads. Here the breads are stuffed with a red kidney bean and caramelized onion paste.

Makes 3

DOUGH

1 egg

100g (3½oz) Homemade Matsoni (see page 29) or natural yogurt

150ml (¼ pint) lukewarm milk

7g (¼oz) fast-action dried yeast

1 teaspoon fine sea salt

½ tablespoon honey

600g (1lb 5oz) plain flour

1 tablespoon sunflower oil, for oiling

GLAZE

1 egg

100g (3½oz) natural yoghurt

FILLING

200g (7oz) dried broad beans ot red kidney beans, soaked overnight in cold water

2 litres (3½ pints) water

2 fresh or dried bay leaves

2 carrots, roughly chopped

2 celery sticks, roughly chopped

5 onions, 1 halved, 4 thinly sliced

100g (3½oz) piece of pancetta rind or smoked streaky bacon (optional)

150g (5½oz) unsalted butter, softened

2 large garlic cloves, finely chopped

sea salt flakes and freshly ground black pepper

To make the dough, mix the egg and the yogurt in a large bowl, then add the yeast, salt and honey. Gradually add the flour, mixing it in first with a spoon and then your hand. You need enough flour so that the dough comes together but is still a little wet. Cover the bowl in clingfilm or a damp tea towel, then leave the dough to rise in the bowl for about an hour. It will double in size and will be very airy, soft and voluptuous.

Meanwhile, drain the soaked beans and add to a saucepan with the water along with the bay leaves, carrots, celery and halved onion. Bring to the boil, skim off the foam that rises to the surface and cook for an hour until the beans are really soft. Add the pancetta rind to the beans for the last 30–40 minutes of the cooking time if you want your beans to have a lovely smoky flavour. If you don't have any pancetta but bacon instead, use in the next step.

continued »

Heat 50g (1¾oz) of the butter – or the bacon, if using, until the fat starts to render – add the thinly sliced onions and cook gently, stirring from time to time, for about 10 minutes until they are deep golden. When they are close to that stage, add the garlic and cook for a few more minutes.

Strain the beans and discard all the vegetables and pancetta rind. Blitz the beans, the onion mixture (leave in the bacon if used) and a little salt and pepper in a blender or food processor. Taste the mixture – it should be sweet and well seasoned. If you wanted to add some of your favourite spices here, such as coriander seeds, toast and then grind them and go ahead, but I like it just as it is.

Divide the dough into 3 pieces. Take one piece of dough and roll it out on a lightly floured work surface into a 30cm (12-inch) round. Take a tablespoonful of soft butter and, using your hand, spread it all over the round. Then fold the right side of the round in and then the left side over it to create a narrow rectangle. If you dare, butter the rectangle again and roll it up. Leave to prove, seam-side down covered with a damp tea towel while you tackle the other two.

To fill the bread, dust the dough and your work surface with flour and roll the dough pieces out into a 20 x 30cm (8 x 12 inch) rectangle. Spread about 200–240g of the bean paste in a thin layer all over each bread. Now roll each piece of dough up into a long sausage and twist into coils to create snail-like shapes. Gently, roll your pin over the snails, to seal the layers together. If your dough is soft, each coil will merge together into a flatbread with a spiral pattern inside. Put them on to separate baking sheets lined with greaseproof paper and leave to prove and expand somewhere cool for an hour, or freeze them to be baked later.

Meanwhile, preheat the oven to 200°C (400°F), Gas Mark 6.

Lightly beat the egg for the glaze and mix in the yogurt and brush over the breads to glaze, then bake for 10–15 minutes. Serve freshly baked with a simple salad for a lunch or quick dinner after work.

Tip Once you are at the stage when the dough has been filled and you have left it to prove, you can freeze it and then glaze and bake at the highest temperature in your oven from frozen.

Opposite: Galiena's shoti (above) and pork lard khachapouri breads.

Ossetian beet top and cheese pies

I grew up with Ossetian pies. Our friend Svetlana is married to an Ossetian and she was taught how to make them by her husband's mother in the mountains, then brought them to Ukraine and wowed us. A pile of them, some with meat, some with cheese, were exotic and familiar at the same time. In Ossetia they are traditionally served three at a time, sometimes round, sometimes triangular, each with a different filling and meant to represent fire, water and earth – most definitely an ancient tradition, originating in paganism. Pagan pies, connecting us with the elements and the universe – I'm in.

Makes 3 large pies (each pie serves 2–3)

OSSETIAN PIE DOUGH

7g (¼oz) fast-action dried yeast

1 teaspoons clear honey

150ml (¼ pint) lukewarm kefir

150ml (¼ pint) lukewarm milk

550g (1lb 4oz) organic white bread flour, plus extra for dusting

1½ teaspoons fine sea salt

BEET TOPS & CHEESE FILLING

20g (¾oz) unsalted butter, plus 50g (1¾oz) for the brown butter, to glaze

350g (12oz) beetroot stalks and leaves (or use Swiss chard)

2 garlic cloves, finely chopped

grated zest of ½ lemon (optional)

200g (7oz) Ogleshield cheese or raclette, coarsely grated

150g (5½oz) feta cheese, crumbled

100g (3½oz) spring onions, chopped

1 tablespoon chopped dill

sea salt flakes and freshly ground black pepper

For the dough, mix the yeast and honey into the lukewarm kefir and milk in a jug and leave for 10 minutes or so until you see bubbles appearing on the surface.

Pour the yeast mixture into a large bowl, then gradually add half the flour and mix together until you have a soft, very wet dough. The reason why we are looking for a very wet dough here is because it will make it easier to add the salt to the dough later – if you add the salt too early, the yeast will struggle to multiply.

Cover the bowl with clingfilm and leave to rise in a warm place for about 40 minutes.

Now make the brown butter to glaze the pies later. Have a heatproof bowl at the ready. Heat the 50g (1¾oz) of butter in a saucepan over a medium-low heat until it starts foaming and then changes colour to deep golden and starts smelling nutty. Immediately tip it from the hot pan into the bowl, otherwise it can continue cooking and may burn. Set aside for later.

Thinly slice the beetroot stalks and roughly chop the leaves. Heat the remaining 20g (¾oz) butter in a pan, add the garlic and cook for a few minutes over a low heat. Then add the beetroot stalks and leaves and cook for a further 5 minutes or so – you are looking for the stalks to soften, but still retain texture. Add the lemon zest at the very end, if using, then give it all a good stir and leave to cool.

Preheat the oven to 220°C (425°F), Gas Mark 7. Line 2 baking sheets with baking parchment.

Once the beet mixture is cool, mix it with the cheeses, season well with salt and pepper and add the spring onions and dill. Mix thoroughly and shape into 3 balls.

Flour your hands, then knead the salt and some of the remaining flour into the risen dough until it stops sticking to your hands. It should still be very soft and pillowy, though. Divide the dough into 3 even pieces. Flatten each piece with your hand and roll out on a lightly floured work surface into rounds about 2cm thick. Place a cheese ball in the centre of each dough round. Bring the edges of the dough up over the filling, pleating as you go, and pinch the ends together really well at the top to secure like a money bag. Sprinkle a little flour over the top and flip the pouch over, then flatten the pouch gently with your hand, spreading the filling inside all the way to the edges. You can also use your rolling pin gently to flatten it a little further.

Pop the pies on to the lined baking sheets. Make a slit in the middle of each pie to let the steam out and bake for 15 minutes. The dough should be golden and the pies' bottoms should be dry. Brush the pies with the brown butter as soon as they are out of the oven and eat immediately.

Try different fillings for your Ossetian pies, using them in the same way as the beet tops and cheese filling (see overleaf)...

continued »

All fillings will fill 3 pies. To scale up or down, you simply need the same weight filling as Ossetian pie dough.

Davondjin... with wild garlic & cheese

20g (¾oz) unsalted butter
500g (1lb 2oz) wild garlic, chopped
200g (7oz) Fresh Homemade Cheese (see page 107) or ricotta cheese (strained if too wet)
200g (7oz) feta cheese, crumbled
sea salt flakes and freshly ground black pepper

Heat the butter in a large frying pan, add the wild garlic and sauté over a low heat for a few minutes, then leave to cool.

Mix the cooled wild garlic with the cheeses, and season well. Divide the mixture into 3 and use to fill the Ossetian pie dough (see page 80).

Kabuskadjin... with shredded cabbage

20g (¾oz) unsalted butter
3 onions, thinly sliced
5 garlic cloves, sliced
3 tablespoons tomato purée
600g (1lb 5oz) sweetheart cabbage, shredded
sea salt flakes and freshly ground black pepper

Heat the butter in a large frying pan, add the onions and cook gently for 10–15 minutes until soft and starting to become golden.

Add the garlic, stir in the tomato purée and cook over a medium heat for a few minutes, then add the cabbage and cook for about 5–8 minutes until the cabbage softens. Leave the mixture to cool, then season well. Divide the mixture into 3 and use to fill the Ossetian pie dough (see page 80).

Baldjin... with sour cherry filling

600g (1lb 5oz) sour cherries, pitted (or use sweet cherries with a squeeze of lemon juice)
300g (3½oz) granulated sugar

Mix the cherries with the sugar. Divide the mixture into 3 and use to fill the Ossetian pie dough (see page 80).

Kartifdjin... with potato & cheese

600g (1lb 5oz) cold leftover mashed potato (with milk and butter)

300g (10½oz) melty cheese, such as Ogleshield or raclette, grated

3 eggs

sea salt flakes, if needed, and freshly ground black pepper

Mix the mashed potato, grated cheese and eggs together really well, then taste and add a little salt if needed and some pepper – you want the mixture to be well seasoned.

Divide the mixture into 3 and use to fill the Ossetian pie dough (see page 80).

Nastdzhyn... with pumpkin, onion & pomegranate molasses

600g (1lb 5oz) butternut squash or pumpkin, peeled, deseeded
and coarsely grated (800g (1lb 12oz) unpeeled weight)

sea salt flakes

4 tablespoons mild olive oil

3 onions, finely diced

5 tablespoons pomegranate molasses

1 tablespoon chopped mint (or other fresh herbs of your choice)

sea salt flakes and freshly ground black pepper

Mix the grated squash or pumpkin with a pinch of salt really well with your hands and set aside.

Heat the oil in a large frying pan, add the onions and sweat until they starting to soften and caramelize.

Add the grated squash or pumpkin to the pan along with the pomegranate molasses, then season to taste. Cook over a medium heat, stirring from time to time, for about 5 minutes until the squash or pumpkin softens.

Leave the mixture to cool, then add the mint. Divide the mixture into 3 and use to fill the Ossetian pie dough (see page 80).

Khinkali

Khinkali is a national Georgian dish. It is said to have originated in the Kazbegi and Tusheti mountains in the northeast, but it is now found all over the country. Normally made with a mixture of beef and pork or lamb, when we visited the hills of Akhaltsikhe, Khatuna and her mother Raya told us that they used to make them using goose meat. Whatever meat you use, the trick is to mince the meat for the filling by hand and to have a rather liquid mixture – the wetter the filling, the more juice each dumpling will contain. Ketino Sujashvili, who lives in the Kazbegi mountains and who taught me this recipe (pictured opposite), screwed the little end off the dough as soon as she shaped the dumpling, but in restaurants, they traditionally leave the tip of the *khinkali* in place so that their guests can niftily hold it in their fingers and discard it while the main bit is eaten. I like the little tip, though, so I don't throw it away. As the dumplings should and will be full of juice inside, be careful not to burn your mouth on the juice or to spill it.

Traditionally, *khinkali* are eaten just with some black pepper ground on top, but I don't bat an eyelid before drizzling them with a little melted butter or even brown butter (see page 80). If you don't finish all of them at one sitting, don't despair. They are not at their best when cold, but are perfect re-fried in a little butter until crispy. Then you could serve them with Tina's Fresh Tkemali (see page 23) or some Satsebeli (see page 19).

Makes 25–30 khinkali

DOUGH

150ml (5fl oz) water

1 tablespoon sunflower oil

300–350g (10½–12oz) plain flour, plus extra for dusting

FILLING

250g (9oz) 50/50 mixture of beef and pork (nice fatty cuts)

150g (5½oz) onion, finely diced

2 small garlic cloves, crushed

100ml (3½fl oz) cold water

¼ teaspoon cayenne pepper

1 green chilli, diced (if you like less heat, leave this out)

1 teaspoon good-quality black peppercorns, freshly ground

sea salt flakes

To make the dough, pour the water and oil into a bowl, then gradually mix in the flour.

Knead the dough on a well-floured work surface for a good 5 minutes, to get the gluten to develop. The dough will be very tight and this is what you want, as it will need to hold quite a substantial filling and you don't want it ripping in the pan. Wrap the dough in clingfilm and leave to rest in the refrigerator for 15–30 minutes, but leave it for longer if possible.

continued »

To make the filling, using a very sharp knife, cut the meat into very thin strips and then cut the strips across. You should end up with very small pieces of meat. You can use a meat cleaver to hand-mince the meat if you are confident with it.

Mix the meat with the onion, garlic, half the measured cold water, the cayenne, green chilli, black pepper and some salt. The pepper is used here as a spice, and you should be able to taste its heat in the resulting *khinkali*. Leave the mixture to stand for about 15 minutes, then add the remaining measured water and leave to stand again for about 10 minutes. If it's your first time, add less water – it will be much easier to practise shaping the dumplings.

Roll out the rested dough on a floured work surface into a 35cm (14-inch) square sheet about 2.5mm (1/10 inch) thick. Bear in mind that you will be rolling the dough out more once the rounds are cut out, and also that you will be using a rather wet and heavy filling, so the dough mustn't be too thin, otherwise the dumplings will burst in the pan. *Khinkali* are sturdy dumplings – there is none of the delicacy of the ethereal *raviolo* here.

Using a glass about 7.5cm (3 inches) in diameter, stamp out rounds from the dough. Roll each round out a little thinner, about 9cm (3½ inches) in diameter.

If making for the first time, start with less filling than you should ideally put in, as it will be easier to practise shaping the dumplings. If you have made them before, place a tablespoonful of the filling in the centre of each round. Using the tips of your fingers, start bringing the edges of the round up over the filling, pleating and pinching firmly as you go, resulting in a money bag shape. Pinch the "neck" of the money bag really well, and either remove the tip or leave it in place. They say that 19 pleats make a truly perfect *khinkali*. I can manage about 12 without straining too much, and that works fine for me. Keep any filled *khinkali* covered with a damp tea towel to prevent them from drying out before cooking.

Bring a large saucepan of salted water to a rolling boil and cook the *khinkali*, in batches of 8, for about 8 minutes – they will float to the top when ready. Remove with a slotted spoon, drain well and serve hot.

VARIATIONS

Khinkali are supposed to be spicy, but if you don't enjoy spice, adjust the flavour to your taste. You can soak the deseeded green chillies in iced water to get rid of some of the heat while retaining the chilli flavour. Ketino added all sorts of beautiful flavourings, such as wild caraway and thyme; or garlic and chopped coriander, although others say that such additions aren't right. But cooking isn't about rules. As long as your *khinkali* are well seasoned and full of juice, they're a winner.

Qutab three ways

Baku has changed. The old Soviet quarters are almost completely destroyed, and we are told that people are forced out of their houses and buildings to make space for companies keen to erect another Dubai-style skyscraper. My brother and I are hopeful that our Aunt's old building is still there. We want to see it – the unusually large balconies, the courtyard, the kids playing chess. Maybe; unlikely. We set off all the same, both determined and hopelessly romantic. A message comes from Aunt Nina saying, "Flat no 1, house 10, Yusuf Zade Street". We check at the hotel and they tell us that all the streets were renamed in the 1990s. This street no longer exists. Rubbish. We run outside and head for the taxi driver with the most silver hair. He only vaguely remembers. "Let's give it a go." We drive into an area that seems to be on the cusp of the sprawling shiny skyscrapers, about to be swallowed up by the modern grandeur within the next few years no doubt. We do not lose hope. Our driver runs out and asks an even more seasoned driver about Yusuf Zade Street. He points at a street that seems to have no ending. We thank them both and set off. Crumbling buildings, washing flapping in the wind, abandoned chairs, more crumbling walls. People keep pointing north; we are at the wrong end of the street. We continue walking and walking. Some of the old Soviet buildings have tiny newly built extensions that serve as little street food stalls/booths. Women keep flipping flatbreads. We must have been walking for over an hour and, now starving, my brother finally makes a decision. Here, we eat here. "What are you making?" I ask. "Kutaby!" *Qutabs* – delicious thin flatbreads stuffed with different fillings – herbs, meat, pumpkin and pomegranates – the options are endless. The woman in a flowery summer dress and headband passes us three of them, fresh and hot, through a barred window, one with soft herbs, one with offal and one with pumpkin. It was one of the best meals we've had in Azerbaijan, hands down. No doubt accentuated by the sense of adventure, nostalgia, a long walk and hunger, but still, it was a snack I will never forget.

Makes 10 medium qutabs (about 75g/2¾oz dough each)
- 200ml (7fl oz) cold water
- 1 egg, lightly beaten
- pinch of fine sea salt

- 500g (1lb 2oz) plain flour, plus extra for kneading and dusting
- 20g (¾oz) unsalted butter, melted (optional)

To make the dough, mix the measured water, egg and salt together in a bowl, then gradually add the flour, combining it with your hand. Tip the dough out on to a well-floured work surface and start kneading it. The dough should be firm but not too dry and should stop sticking to your hands after kneading in some extra flour.

continued »

An extra-large qutab Lizgin-style on the side of the road in Qebele.

Divide the dough into 10 ball-shaped pieces and leave to rest in the refrigerator for 30 minutes, covered with a damp tea towel or clingfilm.

Roll out each piece of dough on a lightly floured work surface as thinly as you can into a 20cm (8-inch) round.

Spread 50g (1¾oz) of the filling on the bottom half of each round, then fold the top half over the filling and pinch the edges together to create a half-moon shape.

Heat a large frying pan until hot – don't use any fat, as we are dry-frying here. Add 1–2 *qutabs* and cook over a medium-high heat for 2–3 minutes on each side until the flatbread is golden and speckled with dark blisters. If you are using a raw meat filling, try to cook the *qutabs* at a slightly lower temperature, making sure that the filling is thoroughly cooked through.

Brush with the melted butter after cooking, if liked.

Tip Some garlicky natural yogurt with mint, a squeeze of lemon juice and a dribble of hot chilli sauce is also delicious served with the qutabs.

Lamb, onion & molasses filling

Some soaked fruit leather (see page 216) is normally used in this filling to add a little acidity, but if you can't make or buy it, simply add some pomegranate molasses instead. Meat provenance is very important here, as the filling is just cooked. This is also lovely when a combination of lamb and beef or beef and pork is used, but of course porkiness is my addition; in primarily Muslim Azerbaijan, it's all about the lamb.

1 recipe quantity of Qutab Dough
(see pages 87–8)

FILLING
350g (12oz) minced lamb (or a 50/50 mix of minced beef and pork)
150g (5½oz) onions, finely diced or grated
1 tablespoon ground cumin
1 tablespoon ground coriander
1 tablespoon dried mint
1 tablespoon pomegranate molasses
1½ teaspoons fine sea salt

TO SERVE
melted unsalted butter, for brushing
ground sumac, for sprinkling

Mix all the ingredients (except the butter and sumac) together.

Test the filling for seasoning by frying a little piece of the mixture in a small pan until cooked through and then tasting – it should be well seasoned.

Use the mixture to fill each dough round and then cook them following the method on page 88.

Brush the cooked *qutabs* with a little melted butter as soon as they come out of the pan and sprinkle over some sumac.

VARIATION
You can also use Kuchmachi (see page 138) to fill the *qutab* dough if you have leftovers – simply chop it really finely before using.

Herb & cheese filling

You can lose the cheese and just up the amount of herbs here, whisking a little egg yolk into the herb filling, but this will make a much thinner layer of filling. You can vary the combination of herbs, or use sorrel instead of some of the herbs, or spinach or even watercress!

continued »

1 recipe quantity of Qutab Dough
(see pages 87–8)

FILLING
400g (14oz) feta cheese, crumbled
100g (3½oz) spring onions, finely chopped
1½ tablespoons chopped dill
1½ tablespoons chopped purple
(or green) basil

1½ tablespoons chopped tarragon
1½ tablespoons chopped coriander
sea salt flakes, to taste, if needed

TO SERVE
melted unsalted butter, for brushing
ground sumac, for sprinkling

Mix all the ingredients (except the butter and sumac) together thoroughly, adding a little salt if the cheese isn't salty enough, using your hands.

Use the mixture to fill each dough round and then cook them following the method on page 88.

Brush the cooked *qutabs* with a little melted butter as soon as they come out of the pan and sprinkle over some sumac.

Squash & pomegranate filling

1 recipe quantity of Qutab Dough
(see pages 87–8)

FILLING
400g (14oz) butternut squash or pumpkin, peeled, deseeded and coarsely grated
2 teaspoons sea salt flakes, plus extra if needed
2 tablespoons mild olive oil
100g (3½oz) onion, finely diced

large handful of pomegranate seeds
1 tablespoon chopped dill
1 tablespoon chopped coriander

TO SERVE
100g (3½oz) natural yogurt
½ garlic clove, crushed
pinch of ground sumac

Mix the grated squash or pumpkin with the salt really well with your hands, then set aside.

Heat the oil in a large frying pan, add the onion and sweat over a medium heat for about 10–15 minutes until starting to soften and caramelize.

Squeeze the liquid out of the grated squash or pumpkin, add it to the frying pan and cook over a low-medium heat, stirring from time to time, for about 5 minutes until softened.

Transfer the mixture to a bowl and leave to cool, then add the pomegranate seeds, herbs and a little more salt if needed. Mix everything together gently so as not to burst the pomegranate seeds.

Use the mixture to fill each dough round and then cook them following the method on page 88. Serve with the yogurt flavoured with the crushed garlic, sprinkled with the sumac.

Aniko's tarragon pie

There are as many versions of this pie as there are women in Georgia, and this recipe from Aniko, the mother of my friend Nino, was a revelation to me. Aniko had kept it a secret her whole life – she wouldn't have revealed it under torture! Nino misses her mum who is now sadly gone, and was unsure about revealing her secret recipe to the thousands of people who may read this book. However, when we met at her childhood home to cook this pie, at midday we were starving and had some cheese, salad and bread along with a drop of wine. When I poured the second shot of wine (we couldn't find bigger glasses), I clumsily overfilled Nino's glass, spilling it all over the tablecloth and the snow-white cheese. Embarrassed, I apologized, but Nino's face lit up, as in Georgia, this is a sign that the ancestors who used to live in the house are happy to receive their descendants and guests. It was a gorgeous omen, making us feel like, finally, mystically, we were allowed to share the recipe.

Serves 6–8

PASTRY

    100g (3½oz) cold unsalted butter, diced, plus extra for greasing

    350g (12oz) plain flour, plus extra for dusting

    100g (3½oz) Homemade Matsoni (see page 29) or kefir or natural yogurt

    2 eggs

    ½ teaspoon fine sea salt

    beaten egg yolk, to glaze

FILLING

4 big bunches of tarragon (about 150g/5½oz), leaves picked and finely chopped

6 spring onions, finely chopped

3 hard-boiled eggs, shelled and chopped

1 teaspoon sea salt flakes, or to taste

2 egg yolks, for glazing

For the pastry, rub the cold butter into the flour in a bowl until it resembles breadcrumbs. Then add the *matsoni* or kefir or yogurt, eggs and salt and mix together well. Knead the dough, adding more flour if the pastry is still too wet – you are looking for a soft but not particularly damp dough. Wrap in clingfilm and leave to rest and firm in the refrigerator for 15 minutes.

Meanwhile, mix all the ingredients for the filling together.

Preheat the oven to 180°C (350°F), Gas Mark 4. Grease a 24cm (9½-inch) round shallow cake tin or pie dish.

Divide the pastry dough in half. Roll out one half on a lightly floured work surface and use it to line the greased tin or dish. Add the filling and spread it evenly over the base of the pastry case. Roll out the other piece of dough, lay it over the top and pinch the edges together. Brush with the beaten egg yolk to glaze and prick it all over with a fork to allow the steam to escape.

Bake the pie for about 20–30 minutes until the pastry is golden and cooked through.

Lavash, chicken & herb pie with barberries

This is an extremely simple dish, taught to me by an Armenian friend, and one of the best ways to turn chicken leftovers into something mind-blowing, although it would be totally worth poaching a whole chicken just to make this. Herbs, seasoned yogurt, barberries, toasted sunflower seeds, chicken, crispy top – I can't think of anything better to eat on a Monday night. If you live alone, or like me with a small child, you can make a mini version using a smaller baking tray.

Serves 6

100g (3½oz) Homemade Matsoni (see page 29) or natural yogurt

2 garlic cloves, grated

pinch of saffron threads (optional)

a pinch of cayenne pepper

1 tablespoon dried barberries (or sultanas)

200g (7oz) poached chicken meat, torn into chunks

1 tablespoon chopped spring onions

1 tablespoon chopped coriander

1 tablespoon chopped dill

1 tablespoon chopped tarragon

50g (1¾oz) unsalted butter, melted

1 large piece of Armenian or Persian lavash (or any other thin flatbread)

1 tablespoon sunflower seeds (or sesame, pumpkin or linseed)

sea salt flakes

Mix the yogurt, garlic, saffron, cayenne and barberries together, then add the chicken, spring onions and herbs. Season well with salt and set aside.

Preheat the oven to 180°C (350°F), Gas Mark 4. Grease a shallow 15 x 20cm (6 x 8 inch) baking dish with some of the melted butter.

Place one layer of lavash in the dish, brush with melted butter then spread over the filling. Cover with another layer of lavash (tear it to fit). Brush with melted butter and sprinkle over the seeds.

Bake for 15 minutes until heated through, the top is golden and the seeds are toasted.

Tip This is a perfect way in which to use up leftover cooked chicken. But it is also a great way to use up stale flatbreads; because you cover them with butter and the filling is so moist, the flatbreads revive beautifully in the oven.

Khingal

We often perceive comfort food as something lovely yet also a little bland, unassuming. It may not blow our minds with flavour, but it gives us that feeling of safe satiety. When I tried *khingal* in the Azerbaijan capital Baku, it was a complete revelation to me. It did all those things that comfort food does, except it also made my eyes widen as my mouth was filled with firm pasta, crispy aromatic lamb and milky, but also oh so fresh, sauce. And then there is the butter. Pasta, spice, butter, crispy meat bits, yogurt, herbs – this dish has every single component that makes me feel safe and yet also titillates my senses, what I imagine a perfect marriage may be like.

Serves 8

1 large egg, lightly beaten

60ml (4 tablespoons) water

200g (7oz) plain flour, plus extra if needed and for dusting

100g (3½oz) Clarified Butter (see page 53) or 60g (2¼oz) unsalted butter and 2 tablespoons vegetable oil, plus extra for cooking the onions

300g (10½oz) coarsely minced lamb

1 teaspoon coriander seeds, lightly toasted and ground

1 teaspoon cumin seeds, lightly toasted and ground

½ teaspoon ground turmeric

2 onions, thinly sliced

200g (7oz) natural yogurt

1 garlic clove, finely grated

a little milk or water

1 tablespoon chopped coriander

1 tablespoon chopped dill

½ teaspoon ground sumac

sea salt flakes and freshly ground black pepper

To make the dough, mix the egg and water together in a bowl, then gradually add the flour (stop if the mixture seems to be getting dry) and knead the mixture in the bowl into a dough. You should end up with a firm, elastic pasta dough, so knead in more flour if it feels too wet. Cover it in clingfilm and leave to rest in the refrigerator for 15–30 minutes.

Preheat the oven to 160°C (325°F), Gas Mark 3, ready for keeping the lamb and onions warm.

Heat half the Clarified Butter or half the ordinary butter and 1 tablespoon oil in a pan. When really hot, add half the minced lamb – you want the meat to be crispy, so overcrowding the pan is not an option here. Fry it without disturbing it too much until it starts crisping up. Add half the spices and some seasoning and cook for 1 minute, then pop into a heatproof bowl and keep warm in the oven.

Repeat with the second batch of meat.

continued »

Don't wipe out the frying pan but add some more butter or oil and cook the onions gently until they become deep golden and luscious. Be patient – it will be worth it. Season them, too, and add them to the lamb keeping warm in the oven.

Roll out the pasta, either by hand or using a pasta machine, but not too thin – about 2mm (1/16 inch) thick – as you want a little bit of a bite here. Then cut the pasta into 3cm (1¼-inch) diamonds. You can let them dry out slightly while you rustle up the yogurt sauce.

You can leave this sauce simple – just mix the yogurt with the garlic and a tiny bit of salt, adding a little milk or water to loosen it up. I also like adding the chopped coriander and dill to it, as well as dusting the whole dish with sumac at the end.

Bring a large saucepan of salted water to the boil and drop in your pasta diamonds. They will be ready within 2 minutes. Check they are cooked by tasting one when they float to the top. Drain them quickly and layer with the meat and onions, drizzling over the yogurt sauce as you go.

Tip *Sometimes I stir a little bit of brown butter (see page 80) into the yogurt. Don't judge me.*

Zeti's kubdari or Svaneti meat pie

Tina is originally from the eastern Georgian region of Kakheti, but she met a Svaneti man, Amiran, and they then moved to Svaneti in the northwest. Tina is a village doctor and walks (she refuses to use a bike or horse) for about six miles every day to work. She also wakes up at 5am each day to milk the cows and does a million other things around the house. Her husband and their Russian friend Sergey, who's lived with them for the past 17 years, work hard on the land. Tina's mother-in-law Zeti taught her how to make this famous Svaneti dish. Hand-chopping the meat is very important here – ready-minced beef just won't have the same level of juiciness. Find some Svaneti salt online to get a flavour as close to the original as possible.

Makes 3

1 recipe quantity of Adjaran Khachapouri dough (see page 103)

organic white bread flour, for dusting

melted unsalted butter, for brushing

FILLING

550g (1lb 4oz) boneless leg or neck of pork

2 mild onions, finely diced

3 garlic cloves, finely chopped

1 teaspoon hot chilli flakes

SPICE MIX

2 tablespoons coriander seeds, ground

1 tablespoon ground blue fenugreek

½ teaspoon black peppercorns, freshly ground

sea salt flakes or Svaneti Salt (see page 63), to taste

Using a very sharp knife (or a meat cleaver if you are comfortable using one), cut the pork into very thin strips and then cut the strips across. You should end up with very small pieces of meat. Combine with the rest of the filling ingredients and 1½ tablespoons of the spice mix.

Preheat the oven to 200°C (400°F), Gas Mark 6.

Divide the dough into 4 pieces, 150g (5½oz) each. Take each piece of dough and, using the back of your hand, stretch it into a thick 15cm (6-inch) round. Place the same weight of filling (150g/5½oz) meat on each round and spread it out. Bring the edges of the dough up over the meat, pleating as you go, and pinch the ends together really well at the top to secure like a money bag. Start flattening the pouch out again with your hands, then sprinkle a little flour over the top and flip it over. Stretch the dough out again with the back of your hand into a 25cm (10-inch) round.

Transfer to large baking sheets and cook in the oven for 15 minutes (you may need to do 2 batches). Brush with some melted butter as soon as it comes out of the oven.

Adjaran khachapouri

This is a meal in itself – a luscious cheesy, eggy, buttery bath to dip the edges of the bread into. I got the original recipe from Arkadiy Petrosyan, a master *acharuli* bread-maker from Batumi on the Black Sea coast. He used an incredibly fresh Imeretian cheese that I found was impossible to source outside Georgia but that you can make yourself (see page 107). Yotam Ottolenghi uses a mixture of ricotta, halloumi and feta, which works a treat, while Nigella Lawson favours feta, mozzarella and ricotta and Felicity Cloake in *The A–Z of Eating* opts for hard mozzarella and feta. I have tried it with my beloved Ogleshield instead of halloumi and its mild dairiness was closer to the original. If you can't find it, try a 2:1 ratio of Edam and Cheddar instead.

Makes 6

DOUGH

7g (¼oz) fast-action dried yeast

2 tablespoons granulated sugar

200ml (⅓ pint) lukewarm water

450g (1lb) organic white bread flour, plus extra for dusting

10g (¼oz) fine sea salt

FILLING

100g (7½oz) full-fat twaróg or ricotta cheese

250g (9oz) Ogleshield or raclette

250g (9oz) feta cheese, crumbled

10g (¼oz) unsalted butter, sliced into 6 pieces

6 small eggs, plus 1 egg yolk

4 whole eggs (or egg yolks)

To make the dough, mix the yeast with the sugar, water, flour and salt in a bowl. Cover the bowl with clingfilm and either leave in the refrigerator overnight or somewhere in your kitchen for an hour or so until doubled in size.

For the filling, mix the cheeses with the single egg yolk and use a fork to mash well.

Preheat the oven to its highest setting and heat a couple of baking sheets – or a pizza stone if you have one.

Flour your work surface really well. Cover your hands in flour and scrape the dough on to your work surface. Knead it in the flour a little if it's too sticky. Divide the dough into 6 pieces (each piece should be about 100g (3½oz)). Roll out each piece of dough on a lightly floured work surface into a 18cm (7-inch) round. Stretch either side of each round to elongate and then pile 100g (3½oz) of filling in the centre, leaving a 5mm (¼ inch) border around the edge. Bring two sides of the dough up to meet in the middle and pinch a seam together to seal, similar to a Cornish pasty. Press down with the flat of your hand to flatten it, then flip it over so the seam is face down. With a sharp knife, make a slash along the middle of the dough and push the sides open to expose the filling. Repeat with the rest of the dough and filling to make 6 khachapouris.

Slide the khachapouris on to the hot baking trays and bake for 10 minutes until the sides turn golden. Crack an egg into the centre of each, then bake for a further 2–3 minutes. To eat, pinch the dough from one end and use it to dip and mix the runny egg yolk into the filling.

Tip In Georgia, the finished article will be served with yet more cubes of butter dropped inside the boats as soon as they come out of the oven. If you have amazing butter and you love it, go ahead. Get your cushions and duvet ready for straight after. Zzzzz.

Tina's khachapouri for a crowd

This is a time saviour and a brilliant way to feed a crowd of people. Instead of making individual *khachapouri*, Tina made this giant version and it worked really well.

Makes 1 large khachapouri

600g (1lb 5oz) Fresh Homemade Cheese (see page 107) or Suluguni (see page 108), or a mixture of feta and ricotta cheese

2 eggs (optional)

sea salt flakes

GLAZE

1 egg yolk

2 tablespoons natural yogurt

DOUGH

200g (7oz) Homemade Matsoni (see page 29) or natural yogurt

1 egg, lightly beaten

2 tablespoons sunflower oil

7g (¼oz) fast-action dried yeast

400g (14oz) plain flour, plus extra for dusting

1 teaspoon fine sea salt

To make the dough, mix the wet ingredients together with the yeast, then mix in the dry ones to make a soft, rather wet dough. Tina, fearlessly, scraped the dough off her hand with the blade of a knife (nothing is wasted). She covers the bowl with a tea towel (or use clingfilm) and leaves it for a minimum of 2 hours in her warm kitchen until doubled in size.

Preheat your oven to its highest temperature.

Divide the dough in half. Tina dusts flour on to a 25 x 35cm (10 x 14 inch) baking tray and puts it on top of her stove to warm up a little. The dough is very, very soft, and she stretches one half of the dough first with her hands and then puts it on to the tray, covering its whole base.

If the cheese is lovely and fatty, as it is in Svaneti, they don't add any eggs. But if your cheese isn't fatty enough, do add the eggs. If it needs it, add some salt to the cheese, then distribute it evenly all over the base dough.

On a well-floured work surface, stretch the remaining dough to the same size of the base dough or as near as possible. Lay it on top of the cheese and make sure you pinch the sides of the two layers of dough together to seal the filling. Mix the egg yolk with the yogurt and use to glaze all over the top, then bake the *khachapouri* for 20–30 minutes until the top is golden and the dough is cooked through.

From right: The Fangani family – Tina, her son and her husband Amiran
with their friend Sergey (far left) beside their Svaneti guest house.

Fresh homemade cheese

In Georgia, a lot of people make this cheese every day. The cheese can either be eaten fresh on the day of making – it's wonderful on toast with Mint Adjika (see page 25) – or left to ripen for a couple of days in the kitchen until it develops large holes. It is then fit for making the salty stretchy cheese known as *sulgun* in Svaneti, or *suluguni* in the rest of Georgia (see page 108). The drained whey shouldn't go to waste, as it can be used for making bread instead of Matsoni (see page 29) or, in Tina's case, for feeding her pregant pig! This is a fun project, and not too difficult.

Makes 400–600g (14oz–1lb 5oz)
- 4 litres (7 pints) raw milk
- 12 teaspoons liquid rennet (or according to the bottle instructions)

TO SERVE
- crushed toasted coriander seeds or chilli flakes (optional)
- sea salt flakes and freshly ground black pepper

You will also need a piece of muslin pressed with a hot iron to sterilize it

Heat the milk in a large saucepan until it is just comfortably warm (like in the cow's udder, Tina tells me). The ideal temperature is 30–40°C (86–104°F) – at 60°C (140°F) it will not be able to curdle, so make sure you don't overheat it.

Add the rennet and stir the mixture for about a minute to make sure the rennet is thoroughly incorporated. Then leave to stand for about an hour until you have what cheesemakers call a 'clean break', where you can hook your forefinger through the set curds and they feel firm, the whey fills the gap and there are few or no curds left on your finger.

The curd should by now separate from the whey. Cut the curds with a balloon whisk a few times and then leave to rest for 20 minutes before scooping out the curds with a slotted spoon. The idea is to increase the surface area of the curds to release more whey, which produces a drier cheese.

Line a fine-mesh sieve with the muslin, add the cheese and leave to drain over a bowl overnight in the refrigerator. Reserve the drained whey for making bread or homemade rennet, or give it to a pregnant pig.

Left in your kitchen at 25°C (77°F), the cheese will ripen and can be used the next day, but if the temperature is higher, you can make the fresh cheese in the morning and in the evening it will be ready for making *suluguni* (see page 108). Serve with the coriander seeds or chilli flakes, if liked.

Suluguni cheese or the "white dollar"

Oh, *suluguni*. It's almost impossible to buy the real deal outside Georgia. The variety you find in Russian delis is, frankly, rubbish – rubbery, tasteless and nothing like the cheese I tried in the Svaneti mountains, made from the milk of the cows that roam the wild slopes and feed themselves rosehips. Tina made this cheese every other day, keeping it in a large hardwood barrel filled with brine. Back in the 1970s, Tina's sister-in-law received many medals for producing record amounts of *suluguni* cheese. Her daily routine involved milking 16 cows every morning and evening, and she did it on her own in record time. They call it "white dollar" in Svaneti, as it is such a premium product (the milk being so excellent and fatty) that they use it as currency! For example, tomatoes and cucumbers come very late in the summer high up in the mountains, but the Svan people need other vegetables, so they exchange *suluguni* for fresh produce – a real bartering system. It can be kept up to a year in brine, becoming rock solid by winter, but that's not a problem, as even grated it's good. They also smoke it in the Samegrelo region once it's hard. *Suluguni* is amazing served with hot sweet tea, hot bread or with boiled potatoes, or just with bread and tomatoes. The Georgians add it to *gomi* (Georgian polenta). They often use fresh cheese to fill *khachapouri*, but grated *suluguni* also works really well.

Makes 300g (10½oz)

600g (1lb 5oz) Fresh Homemade Cheese (see page 107)

SATURATED BRINE

2 litres (3½ pints) natural spring or still mineral water (not tap water)

750g (1lb 10oz) sea salt flakes, plus extra for sprinkling the stretched cheese

STORING BRINE

2 litres (3½ pints) natural spring or still mineral water

300g (10½oz) salt

You will also need 2 large saucepans, a heavy-duty plastic container and a sterilized airtight plastic container

For the saturated brine, pour the water into a large saucepan, add the salt and heat, stirring, until the salt has completely dissolved. Set aside.

Make the storing brine in the same way, then pour into a heavy-duty plastic container and set aside.

To ripen your fresh cheese, place it in a sterilized airtight plastic container and leave it at room temperature for about 36 hours until holes appear in the cheese, which you need in order for it to melt, otherwise the cheese will be too granular in texture to melt.

Cut the ripe fresh cheese into 2.5cm (1-inch) slices. Bring a 2-litre (3½-pint) saucepan of water to a steady gentle simmer and add the cheese. It will float in the water, so keep it submerged with a spoon until it starts to melt, after about 30 seconds or so. Then squeeze the cheese to check when it changes from airy to granular and then to putty-like in consistency. Once it looks like shiny putty, it should be possible to fold/stretch it without it falling apart.

Take the cheese out and stretch and fold it a few times like you would with dough (you need asbestos hands here, or protect your hands by wearing thin latex gloves). Dip it back in the hot water periodically for a few seconds to help keep it workable. If easier, work on a couple of pieces at a time and then put them together (heating as needed) into a rope to stretch and then to form a ball.

Put the folded cheese into a bowl or another pan. Tina then adds a light sprinkling of salt on top of the cheese. Leave the cheese to stand in the kitchen for a maximum of 12 hours.

Add the cheese to the saturated brine and leave for a couple of hours, then transfer to the storing brine and keep in a cool place. You can use the *suluguni* after 2 days' soaking in the brine.

Tips

Some Georgian families keep the brine for a few years and just replenish it with salt after adding new cheese, every three weeks, as it absorbs the salt from the water. Tina changes her brine only once a year.

If your **suluguni** *goes really hard and salty, just use it like you would* **ricotta salata** *– finely grated over some pasta, or grated over a chopped salad instead of feta.*

Dyushbara

A really skilled cook is able to make these dumplings so small that 10–15 of them will fit on one tablespoon. Some may think this is showing off, but Azerbaijans tell me it is their ultimate expression of hospitality. As much as I love these dumplings really really small, I am personally too greedy, as well as too lazy, so I make 5cm (2-inch) jumbo *dyushbara*. But feel free to up them to 8cm (3¼ inches) in size if you think your life is too short for faffing around with tiny pasta. They still cook within minutes and have a little bit more substance. The dumplings are normally served with only a couple of the items listed, for example just the mint and garlic vinegar. But if I am cooking for a lot of people or for guests at home, I love bringing out a whole row of small dishes, allowing for a fun flavour DIY dining experience. I, of course, add a little bit of everything, being greedy.

Serves 6

sea salt flakes and freshly ground black pepper

CHICKEN STOCK

2 chicken carcasses or 1 medium organic chicken, cut into pieces

1 onion, halved

2 celery sticks, chopped

2 carrots, scrubbed and chopped

2 dried bay leaves, crumbled

PASTA DOUGH

1 egg, lightly beaten

60ml (4 tablespoons) water

200g (7oz) plain flour, plus extra for dusting

FILLING

100g (3½oz) minced lamb

100g (3½oz) minced pork

½ teaspoon ground cumin

½ teaspoon ground coriander

½ carrot, scrubbed and finely grated

1 small onion, finely diced or coarsely grated

TO SERVE

2 tablespoons chopped coriander

2 tablespoons chopped tarragon

2 tablespoons chopped dill

2 tablespoons chopped purple basil

2 teaspoons dried mint

2 teaspoons ground sumac

50ml (2fl oz) good-quality vinegar (white wine or cider will be perfect), infused with 1 small garlic clove, crushed

Throw all the stock ingredients into a large stockpot and cover with cold water, about 3 litres (5¼ pints). Bring to the boil, skim off the scum and cook for 1½ hours, or longer if you have time. If you are using a good chicken, remove it after an hour and leave it to cool a little, then take the meat off the bones and save for another recipe (see Tip, overleaf). Return the chicken carcass and bones to the pot and keep cooking until reduced by one-third.

continued »

flour & ash   111

Strain the stock, discarding all the vegetables, bay and chicken bones. You should end up with 1.8–2 litres (3¼–3½ pints) stock. Season it really well with salt.

To make the pasta dough, mix the egg and measured water together in a bowl, then gradually add enough flour to form a firm dough.

Knead the dough on a well-floured work surface until it stops sticking to your hands. You should end up with firm, elastic dough. Wrap it in clingfilm and leave to rest in the refrigerator for at least 20 minutes.

Roll out the dough on a lightly floured work surface as thinly as you can into a sheet about 40cm (16 inches) square; if using a pasta machine, keep rolling it through the settings until you reach the second to thinnest setting (thin, but thick enough not to rip under the weight of the filling).

Cut the sheet into strips so that you end up with small squares. If they are as little as 1.5cm (⅝ inch), you may mildly impress an Azerbaijani person. If you don't have an Azerbaijani friend to impress, don't worry and cut the dough into 5cm (2-inch) squares for jumbo *dyushbara* dumplings. They should, however, remain relatively small, as the meat filling is raw and so must cook through before the pasta becomes overdone. But if the dumpling is too small, it loses appeal to me – I need to have a good mouthful of pasta and filling to be truly satisfied.

Mix all the filling ingredients together well, seasoning with salt and plenty of pepper.

Place about ½ teaspoon of the filling on each pasta square, fold in half and pinch the edges firmly together. Then take 2 opposite corners and pinch them together. I prefer pinching them so that they look like little fish tails.

Bring a large pan of salted water to the boil, then add the dumplings, in small batches, and cook for 1–2 minutes until they float to the surface. The reason why I don't cook them in the stock is that I don't want the stock to become starchy and cloudy, but if your dumplings are not heavily floured, you can cook them in the boiling stock.

Serve the dumplings in the hot stock, with all or a selection of the fresh and dried herbs and the garlicky vinegar alongside, as you wish.

Tip *If you used a whole chicken to make the stock, you could use the chicken meat to make Lavash, Chicken & Herb Pie with Barberries (see page 96).*

Khanuma

Variations of this dish exist all over the Caucasus and Central Asia. It reminds me of *beshbarmak*, a pasta, lamb and onion dish that is so invitingly slippery, you hardly have to chew any of it, as it simply disappears when your fork or preferably your fingers reach your mouth. It's incredibly satisfying. Just think onions caramelized in chicken fat and then wrapped in thin pasta dough, served with a chicken broth flavoured with saffron and a ton of herbs. This dish will nourish or cure, or seduce someone to fall in love with you, with just seven main ingredients.

Serves 6

- 1 medium well-fed (you need the fat!) organic chicken
- a few spare vegetables, such as celery, leeks or carrots, chopped (optional)
- 2 onions, thinly sliced
- 2 eggs
- 1 tablespoon water

- 150g (5½oz) "00" pasta flour or plain flour, plus extra for dusting
- pinch of saffron threads
- large handful of soft herbs of your choice, such as dill, coriander, basil or tarragon, chopped
- sea salt flakes

Cut all the visible fat off the chicken – it often has lots all around the cavity – and reserve.

Pop the chicken (you can joint it first if you like, or just use it whole) into a large saucepan and cover with water – about 3 litres (5¼ pints). Bring to a simmer, skim off the scum and add some salt. If you have some vegetables hanging around, add those as well for extra flavour. Simmer for about an hour until the chicken is really tender.

Meanwhile, put the reserved chicken fat in a deep frying pan and slowly heat it until it starts to sizzle. Add the onions, lightly season them with salt and cook slowly over a low heat for about 15 minutes until they turn deep golden. Leave them to cool a little.

To make the dough, mix the eggs and measured water together in a large bowl with a fork, then gradually add 100g (3½oz) of the flour and knead it into a firm dough, first in the bowl, then on the work surface until smooth. Knead in the remaining 50g (1¾oz) of flour if the dough is too wet. Cover the bowl with clingfilm and leave the dough to rest in the refrigerator for about 15 minutes, but up to 1 hour if you can.

Roll out the dough on a lightly floured work surface as thinly as you can. Tip the onions and the melted chicken fat on top of the rolled-out dough and roll it up tightly into a long sausage, then twist the sausage as if you are trying to wring out some wet laundry. Cut the twisted roll into 6cm (2½-inch) pieces.

Don't wash the onion pan out, as there will be lots of flavour clinging to its sides, but add about 1 litre (1¾ pints) water to it and some salt – it should be well seasoned. Bring to the boil, add the pasta rolls and simmer them for about 5 minutes until tender.

Strain the chicken broth, reserving the chicken but discarding the vegetables if you used any.

Grind your saffron with the sea salt flakes using a pestle and mortar, then mix in a ladleful of the broth and pour the saffron liquid back into the soup pan. Taste and adjust the seasoning.

To serve, place some pieces of chicken meat and a couple of rolls in each soup plate, pour in a little bit of the broth and sprinkle over the herbs. Seductive cooking.

Mum always laughs about what she calls Georgian, "greyhound pigs", long-legged and lean, left to roam free, splashing in puddles. Despite animals being everywhere (in western Georgia the cow owns the road), we did not sample many meat dishes travelling through Georgia and Azerbaijan. Of course, meat is easily available, but people who take care of their own pigs and cows rarely eat it – only when the season is right. This is what my grandparents did in Ukraine. Meat was a rarity, a luxury, which is what it is supposed to be in my opinion. I still live by these rules, eating mostly vegetables, and, if indulging in meat, eating head to tail (I will never sniff at giblets or tails). I buy meat of the highest quality which guarantees the animal had a good life. I think they call it "flexitarian" these days. I call it "way of life as it should be, and now more than ever".

beasts from land, sea & air

Chicken chigyrtma

There are so many ways to extract flavour from saffron. Some advise pouring hot water over it; some say to grind it with salt with a pestle and mortar. My friend Zulya instructed me to soak it in a bowl of warm water (hot water kills the flavour, she says), with the bowl standing on a warm surface.

Serves 6–8

100g (3½ oz) Clarified Butter (see page 53)

1 small organic chicken, cut into 10 pieces

4–5 onions, not too thinly sliced

pinch of ground turmeric

pinch of saffron threads, soaked in 50ml (2fl oz) warm water for 5 minutes with the bowl standing on a warm surface

50ml (2fl oz) verjuice or lemon juice

1 tablespoon granulated sugar

6 eggs

1 tablespoon natural yogurt

Saffron Plov, to serve (see page 120); Zulya's Plov Condiment (see page 121) and any other dishes you like such as Pickled Cherries & the Gang (see page 186)

Heat the Carified Butter in a large pan and brown the chicken pieces, in batches, really well. Set aside.

Add the onions to the pan and fry over a medium heat for about 10 minutes until they are light golden, then stir in the turmeric, the saffron and its soaking water, verjuice or lemon juice and sugar.

Return all the chicken to the pan, cover with a lid and cook for 10–15 minutes. Then turn off the heat and leave to cool.

Preheat the oven to 180°C (350°F), Gas Mark 4.

Beat the eggs and yogurt together.

Pack the chicken and onions snugly into a baking dish and pour over the egg mixture, then prod all over with a spoon so that the egg mixture is evenly distributed. Bake for 35 minutes until golden and crispy on top, then serve as part of a bigger feast.

Saffron plov

This is one of the most head-spinningly fragrant and buttery *plovs* that I know. It is traditionally served with Chicken *Chigyrtma* (see previous page), but it is such a show-stopper of a dish that I love serving it with pretty much any meat or vegetarian dish, its flavours working especially well with saffron, nuts and dried fruit. I adore how two of my favourite cuisines, Persian and Turkish, marry in Azerbaijan. Azerbaijani *plovs* are similar to Iranian in that they both feature the delicious crispy bottom, called *gazmakh* in Azerbaijan and *tahdig* in Farsi. However, Iranians don't cover their *plovs* in melted clarified butter; pouring melted butter over everything is a Turkic influence, and in my opinion it's not a bad influence either! My friend Zulfiya used cornel cherries here but you can substitute with dried barberries or sour cherries.

Serves 6–8

about 200g (7oz) Clarified Butter (see page 53)

a good pinch of saffron threads, plus 3 small pinches

350g (12oz) premium basmati rice, soaked in heavily salted cold water for 2 hours and rinsed well

50g (1¾oz) flaked almonds

50g (1¾oz) pistachio nuts, roughly chopped

4 tablespoons sultanas

2 tablespoons ready-to-eat dried apricots, thinly sliced

2 tablespoons dried barberries or sour cherries

50ml (2fl oz) water

150g (5½oz) natural yogurt

1 small egg

sea salt flakes

Melt 100g (3½oz) of the Clarified Butter in a pan, add the good pinch of saffron and leave to stand in a warm place for 10 minutes or so.

Fill a large pan with water, add loads of salt so that it's as salty as seawater and bring to a rolling boil. Add the rice to the water, then wait for it to boil furiously, stirring once. Boil for 7 minutes until al dente, almost ready. Drain it really well, then tip it on to a large baking tray and spread it out to make sure that it's not in one big pile, otherwise it will overcook.

Melt 2 tablespoons of the Carified Butter in a frying pan and toast the flaked almonds and pistachios separately, in batches. Save for garnishing later.

Soak each of the dried fruits separately in the measured water and a small pinch of saffron for a few minutes. Then tip all the dried fruit and the soaking water into a pan with a tablespoon of the Clarified Butter and cook until the water evaporates. Once that has happened, fry them in the same pan over a high heat for a minute.

Put a couple of tablespoons of melted Clarified Butter into a large, heavy-based saucepan. Beat the yogurt, egg, some salt and a further 2 tablespoons of melted Clarified Butter together with 3 tablespoons of the cooked rice until well combined. Spread the mixture evenly over the base of the pan. "Pour" the rice over gently, keeping it loose and not packing it down, then drizzle over the Clarified Butter and saffron infusion. Cover with a lid wrapped in a damp tea towel.

Place the pan over a high heat until you hear a "pshshshsht" sound when you touch the "bum of the pan", as Zulfiya has so playfully put it (she does it with a finger, but do it with a wet tea towel). Now reduce the heat to the lowest flame possible and cook for about 40 minutes.

Once the time is up, wet a tea towel and lay it on a chopping board, then stand the hot pan on top. Spoon the rice on to a platter. Then using a wooden spoon, gently lift out the crispy bit on the bottom (the *gazmakh*) and break it into pieces or cut it up and scatter it on top of the rice. Decorate the *plov* with the toasted nuts and dried fruit (see photo on page 118).

Zulya's plov condiment

Serves 6–8

50g (1¾oz) Clarified Butter (see page 53)

2 onions, diced

1 quince, cored and diced

60g (2¼oz) sultanas

5 tablespoons water

seeds of 1 pomegranate

pinch of saffron threads, soaked in 50ml (2fl oz) warm water for 10 minutes with the bowl standing on a warm surface

sea salt flakes

Heat the Clarified Butter in a saucepan, add the onions, season with salt and fry over a medium heat for about 10 minutes until they are golden and soft.

Add the quince, sultanas and 2 tablespoons water, cover the pan with a lid and cook over a low heat for 15 minutes until the quince and sultanas have absorbed all the water.

Stir in the pomegranate seeds and saffron and its soaking water along with the remaining water and stir really well, then cover again and cook for a further 6 minutes.

Turn off the heat and leave to infuse for about 15 minutes before serving.

Nazilya's cholme kiabab

Zulfiya's Aunt Nazilya from Lankaram is the most incredible cook. She uses a gorgeous plum and walnut stuffing for both fish and chicken – this one is a real classic. This is originally a grilled dish, as whole birds are often cooked in tandyr (tandoori-style) ovens in Azerbaijan.

Serves 4–6
  1 small organic chicken
  2 tablespoons Alycha paste (*tursha*) or tamarind paste (any tart, fruity paste will do)
  1 recipe quantity of Fish Lavangi Winter Filling (see page 160)
  100ml (3½fl oz) water

Rub the chicken with the Alycha or tamarind paste, season with some salt, then stuff the cavity with the lavangi filling, spreading some all over the chicken. You may need to secure the cavity with a couple of wooden cocktail sticks so that the filling doesn't spill out.

Pop the chicken breast side down into a large pan and add the water. Cover the pan with a lid and cook over a gentle heat for an hour, turning the bird over halfway through. The liquid should have reduced into a sticky, slightly tart and flavoursome sauce.

Vine leaf dolma

I tried this recipe using a mysterious preserved leaf I found at a market in Baku. The woman convinced me that what I was buying was *lipa* or linden tree leaves, but I think they were actually young quince leaves. I was surprised to discover how many different leaves can be used for stuffing, although the more easily available vine leaves are fine to use here.

Makes 28

2 tablespoons vegetable oil

2 large onions, finely diced

½ carrot, scrubbed and roughly grated

1 tablespoon chopped coriander

1 tablespoon chopped mint

1 tablespoon chopped dill

2 teaspoons ground cumin

2 teaspoons ground coriander

1 teaspoon fennel seeds, toasted and ground

400g (14oz) boneless, fatty cut of beef and 400g (14oz) skinless pork belly, coarsely minced together (ask your butcher to prepare)

200g (7oz) basmati rice, parboiled and cooled

300g (10½oz) fresh vine leaves or 500g (1lb 2oz) preserved

500ml (18fl oz) chicken or other meat or vegetable stock

sea salt flakes and freshly ground black pepper

natural yogurt, seasoned with a tiny bit of crushed garlic, a pinch of ground cinnamon and salt, to serve

Heat the oil in a large frying pan, add the onions and cook gently for about 15 minutes until they soften and start becoming golden. Add the grated carrot and cook over a higher heat, stirring from time to time, for 3–5 minutes until that, too, begins to caramelize. Add the herbs and spices and cook over a medium heat for a further minute.

Leave the vegetable mixture to cool, then mix it with the minced meat and the rice. Season with salt and pepper.

Blanch the vine leaves – the fresh ones only need to see the water for 10 seconds or so; the preserved leaves 2 minutes.

Go through the vine leaves, and if there are some that are damaged or seem too tough, don't throw them away but layer them over the base of a flameproof casserole dish that you will be cooking your *dolma* in.

To assemble the *dolma*, lay the first vine leaf for stuffing in front of you on your work surface, rough side up and shiny side down, with the point of the leaf facing away from you.

continued »

Take a tablespoon of the meat mixture and place it at the base of the leaf. Fold the right side of the leaf in over the meat mixture, then do the same with the left side. Starting from the base, roll up the leaf. Repeat with the rest of the vine leaves and meat, tucking the rolls next to each other in the casserole dish. You might get two layers out of them depending on the size of your casserole.

Pour the stock over the *dolma* and cover with a plate or something a little smaller in diameter than the casserole dish, then add a heavy weight on top, such as a can. The *dolma* should be submerged in the stock, but there should be about 2cm (¾ inch) of space left above in the pan so that the bubbling stock doesn't escape from the pan.

Cook the *dolma* over a low heat, uncovered, for about 1¼ hours. If there is still a lot of liquid left once the cooking time is up, turn the heat up and cook until reduced. Serve the *dolma* warm with some of the reduced pan juice drizzled over, along with the seasoned yogurt.

VARIATION
I've tried this recipe with interesting grains, like siyez and freekeh. Just use them in exactly the same way as the rice.

Summer filling

2 tablespoons vegetable oil

2 onions, finely diced

½ carrot, scrubbed and roughly grated

½ bunch of tarragon, chopped

½ bunch of dill, chopped

½ bunch of mint, chopped

2 tablespoons chopped basil

1 tablespoon chopped coriander

1 tablespoon chopped flat leaf parsley

1 teaspoon rubbed mint

½ bunch of spring onions, finely diced

800g (1lb 12oz) fatty minced lamb

200g (7oz) rice, parboiled, well drained and cooled

300g (10½oz) fresh vine leaves or 500g (1lb 2oz) preserved

500ml (18fl oz) chicken or other meat or vegetable stock

sea salt flakes and freshly ground black pepper

Follow the method above, adding the spring onions with the herbs.

Kharcho

Ia, the school head teacher in Megrelia (Samegrelo), taught me how to make the real deal *kharcho*. It is not a soup but a hearty stew in western Georgia, so delicious I could drink the sauce on its own. Ia says that the original version was always made with chicken, but since it has become so popular around Georgia beef has been used, and as the beef version is considered better, it has become the go-to meat to use for this dish. They serve it with *gomi* (Georgian polenta) in Samegrelo, but it would be equally nice with polenta, plain rice or any other carb you love.

Serves 4–6

1kg (2lb 4oz) beef shin or any other fatty beef, cut into large chunks

3 onions, roughly chopped

1 bunch of coriander, leaves, stalks and roots (if the latter are available, well washed)

150g (5½oz) good-quality walnuts

2 tablespoons Red Adjika Salt (see page 62; or see Tip below) or chilli paste

2 teaspoons ground blue fenugreek

1½ tablespoons tomato purée

3 large garlic cloves, crushed

a few pomegranate seeds (optional)

Put the meat into a saucepan and pour over enough cold water to cover by 5cm (2 inches). Cook over the lowest heat possible for about 1½ hours, skimming off the scum from time to time. It should start becoming soft, ready to fall apart but not quite.

Meanwhile, blitz the onions, coriander stalks and roots (reserve the leaves), walnuts, *adjika* salt (or chilli paste) and blue fenugreek in a blender or food processor.

Skim a little bit of the fat off the beef stock and spoon it into a small saucepan. Stir in the tomato purée and cook for 2 minutes, then add the onion and walnut paste. Cook over a low heat for about 15 minutes, stirring often. If it becomes too dry, keep adding more beef fat.

Remove the meat from the stock and pull it off the bone. Increase the heat under the stock and reduce it to about 400ml (14fl oz). Add the pulled meat back into the stock, reduce the heat and add the onion and walnut paste. Taste, and if you used the Red Adjika Salt you may not need more salt. But add more if it needs it. Add the crushed garlic and cook for 1 minute.

Chop some of the coriander leaves roughly and serve sprinkled on top. A few pomegranate seeds would also be nice if you have some.

Tip Having the heat of Red Adjika Salt here is quite important. But if you can't find or make it, whip up this alternative. Blitz 2 long red chillies with 5 peeled garlic cloves, 1 teaspoon coriander seeds and 1 tablespoon sea salt flakes in a blender or food processor. Use in moderation, as this is essentially a wet flavoured salt.

Shakh plov

It never ceases to surprise me how far and wide Yotam Ottolenghi's influence has reached all around the world. Zulya is a big admirer of his and she told me that her outstanding version of (generally much simpler) Shakh Plov was inspired by Ottolenghi's quinoa and rice recipe. This is a regal dish, fit for a prince – or your dinner party guests. Cut into the sonorous lavash crust at the table and let the jewelled filling spill out on to a tray. It is actually relatively easy to make, but it will look like you have been slaving all day to produce something this beautiful. This is a meal in itself, so simply serve with a few bunches of soft herbs like mint, dill, coriander and purple basil along with some flavoursome sliced cucumbers and tomatoes in the summer, or with pickled vegetables in winter (see pages 179–186). Do play around with the filling, too – you can use slow-cooked and gently spiced shredded lamb instead of chicken, or make it vegetarian by substituting briefly roasted pumpkin pieces for the meat.

Serves 6–8

300g (10½oz) Clarified Butter (see page 53)

800g (1lb 12oz) boneless, skinless organic chicken thighs

good pinch of saffron threads

50ml (2fl oz) cold water

200g (7oz) banana shallots, sliced

1 teaspoon cumin seeds, lightly toasted and ground

80g (3oz) flaked almonds, lightly toasted

50g (1¾oz) dried sour cherries or dried barberries, or a mixture of both

30g (1oz) ready-to-eat dried apricots, sliced

30g (1oz) sultanas

350g (12oz) premium basmati rice, soaked in heavily salted cold water for 2 hours and rinsed well

15 x 20cm (8-inch) thin lavash flatbreads

sea salt flakes and freshly ground black pepper

You will also need a deep ovenproof pan 26–28cm (10½–11 inches) in diameter with a lid

Heat 1 tablespoon of the Clarified Butter in a large frying pan and cook the chicken thighs, in batches, over a medium-high heat until golden all over but not necessarily cooked through. Set the chicken aside, but don't worry about cleaning the pan, as you will be cooking the shallots in it.

To prepare the saffron, add to the measured water in a bowl and leave to stand on a warm surface – they are cautious with saffron in Azerbaijan, believing that soaking it in hot water kills its flavour.

Melt a few more tablespoons of the Clarified Butter in the frying pan and cook the shallots until soft and lightly caramelized.

Shred the chicken, then add it to the caramelized shallots with the saffron and its soaking water and season well with salt and pepper. Stir in the cumin, flaked almonds and dried fruit, then cover the pan with a lid and cook over a low heat for 5 minutes. Turn off the heat and leave it to cool down a bit.

Meanwhile, fill a large pan with water, add loads of salt and bring to a rolling boil. Add the rice to the boiling water, then wait for it to boil furiously, stirring once. Boil for 7 minutes until al dente, then drain it thoroughly. They use massive colanders in Azerbaijan with a surface area large enough to allow the rice to cool down properly, but instead you can tip the rice on to a large baking tray and spread it out so that the steam escapes and the rice doesn't overcook.

Preheat the oven to 180°C (350°F), Gas Mark 4.

Brush most of the lavash, one by one, with the remaining melted Clarified Butter – or dip into the butter in a bowl, as they do in Azerbaijan(!), then use to line the base and sides of the deep ovenproof pan, allowing enough overhanging the sides to cover the top when folded over. Build up 3 layers of the lavash with no holes showing, using your judgement as to how many lavash you want to dip into the butter, as you want it all to be buttery but not completely soaking.

Using a large spoon, add the chicken mixture to the lavash pan and then add the rice mixture gently so that it's not tightly packed in. Carefully fold the overhanging lavash over the rice to encase it.

Cover the pan with the lid and bake for 40 minutes. Then lower the oven temperature to 160°C (325°F), Gas Mark 3, remove the lid and bake for a further 10 minutes so that the top crisps up.

Using a thick tea towel, very carefully (as some butter might splatter you) tip the *plov* on to a plate. You should have something that looks like a gorgeous, crispy-skinned pie. Leave it to stand for 5 minutes before cutting it. You should hear a very satisfying crunchy sound.

Quince stuffed with lamb & caramelized shallots

Dolma comes in so many forms. In fact, anything stuffed with a bit of meat and rice can actually be called *dolma*, or *tolma* in Armenian, including aubergines, peppers, tomatoes, potatoes, vine leaves, quince leaves (!) and quince itself. To me, quince is the queen of fruit. Astringent, tannic and sour when raw (try thin, raw slices sprinkled with salt and sumac), it becomes the most luxuriously tasting aromatic thing when cooked. And despite being very sweet, it lends itself so naturally to savoury fillings. Look for it in Turkish shops come the autumn, and do not give this dish a miss. Serve it with a simple chicory and pomegranate salad.

Serves 2

4 ripe quinces

2 tablespoons olive oil

400g (14oz) coarsely minced lamb

2 teaspoons coriander seeds, toasted and crushed

2 teaspoons fennel seeds, toasted and crushed

2 teaspoons cumin seeds, toasted and crushed

15g (½oz) unsalted butter

6 shallots, sliced

sea salt flakes and freshly ground black pepper

Preheat the oven to 200°C (400°F), Gas Mark 6.

Slice the quinces in half lengthways and remove the cores, scooping out quite a bit of the flesh in order to be able to fit in the lamb.

Place the quince halves cut side up on a baking tray. Drizzle over and rub in 1 tablespoon of the oil and sprinkle over some salt and a little pepper. Cover with foil and bake for 30 minutes.

Meanwhile, heat the other tablespoon of oil in a frying pan and fry the lamb over a high heat for a few minutes along with the spices and some salt and pepper. Take the meat out and set aside.

Add the butter and the shallots to the pan, lower the heat and cook them slowly until they soften and start turning golden. This can take up to 15 minutes.

Remove the foil from the quince and bake for a further 15 minutes.

Stuff the baked quinces with the lamb mixture and top with the shallots. Return to the oven for about 10 minutes until the quince is soft. Your house will be permeated with a sweet, warming aroma.

Poussin tabaka in blackberry sauce

Georgians love treating their fruit in a serious, savoury way. Plums, grapes, mulberries – they all turn delectably savoury with the addition of some garlic, salt and strong soft herbs. Blackberries that are small and intense in flavour go really beautifully with chicken. In my first cookbook *Mamushka*, I give the classic *tabaka* recipe and explain that the word *tabaka* comes from *tapa*, a special cast-iron pan traditionally used for cooking spatchcocked chickens, which were then covered in garlic oil. This recipe is the "next level" *tabaka*. You will experience savoury fruitiness here in a new, thrilling, even mind-blowing way. Duck and its orange should take a break.

Serves 4

2 poussins (or 1 small organic chicken)

1 tablespoon vegetable oil

30g (1oz) unsalted butter

100g (3½oz) grapes

300g (10½oz) blackberries

1 tablespoon verjuice or pomegranate molasses

2 garlic cloves, crushed

½ teaspoon cayenne pepper

1 teaspoon chopped marjoram or oregano

1 tablespoon chopped coriander stalks

a tiny amount of dill

sea salt flakes and freshly ground black pepper

To spatchcock the birds, place each bird, breast side down, on a chopping board, and, using sharp kitchen scissors or a knife, cut along either side of the backbone. Then turn the bird over and flatten with the palm of your hand.

Season the birds very well with salt and pepper.

Heat the oil and butter in a large frying pan. Add the poussins cut side down and make sure you brown those bones, as this will add tons of flavour.

Now flip the birds cut side up and cook over a medium-high heat for about 5 minutes to develop a bit of colour. Cover with a cartouche (a circle of baking parchment or greaseproof paper) with another, slightly smaller frying pan on top and then add a heavy weight, such as a can or heavy mortar and pestle. Cook over a very low heat for 25 minutes.

Meanwhile, make the sauce. If have managed to source the unripe sour grapes, blitz them with the blackberries in a blender or food processor, or use a pestle and mortar if you want to be romantic about it, then pass through a sieve into a saucepan.

Add the verjuice or pomegranate molasses and cook for a few minutes, then add the garlic, cayenne pepper and marjoram or oregano and cook for a further 10 minutes. Finally, add the coriander stalks to the sauce with the dill.

The poussins should be ready now, but check that the juices run clear when you pull at the legs. Take them out of the pan and leave to rest for a few minutes. You can mix the juices from the poussins through the sauce for extra lusciousness if you like. Pour the sauce over the birds and serve with a simple salad and a chunk of good bread.

Chicken satsivi

Both Ia and Nino make really special examples of *satsivi*, which I sampled in Georgia, so this recipe is the result of my taking the favourite bits from both. This is a festive dish, one that nobody would cook on an everyday basis because, even though walnuts grow in abundance in Georgia, they are expensive. I like to use this sauce as I would tahini. Turkey *satsivi* is a typical Christmas dish and it's a true wonder. As cooks, we are rarely faced with dealing with unplucked birds in the West, but this is how they would come in the Caucasus. On one occasion, Nino travelled with her dad from Baku to Tbilisi and they sat next to a couple of Azerbaijani women, live turkeys in hand. Conversation flowed and recipes were exchanged. What was particularly interesting, though, was the method that the women used to pluck their unfortunate birds. Instead of pouring boiling water on the skin, like Nino's mum used to do, they reported that they wrapped the (thankfully dead!) critters in wet muslin and ran over them with an iron. Nino tried it the following Christmas and never looked back. It is equally effective with large game birds, apparently. But... maybe don't try this at home.

Serves 4–6

1 medium organic chicken, plus a bunch of chicken bones (ask your butcher)

2 small onions or 4 shallots, peeled and halved

vegetable oil, for oiling the chicken

200g (7oz) dried walnuts (see Tip)

2 large cloves garlic, grated

1 teaspoon Red Adjika Salt (see page 62) (optional)

½ tablespoon *khmeli-suneli* spice mix (see page 226)

1 teaspoon chopped coriander

pinch of cayenne pepper

sea salt flakes and freshly ground black pepper

Put the chicken bones and a small pinch of salt into a saucepan and add about 1 litre (1¾ pints) cold water or enough to just cover. If there is a little bit of loose fat on your chicken, add that as well. Cook over a low heat for an hour until the liquid has reduced by half to about 500ml (18fl oz). At first, skim off the scum, but then keep skimming the fat that rises to the surface and reserve it.

Meanwhile, preheat the oven to 200°C (400°F), Gas Mark 6.

Place the onion or shallot halves in a roasting tray with the reserved chicken fat, season well with salt and roast for 20–30 minutes until they become soft and slightly caramelized. Remove from the oven.

Reduce the oven temperature to 180°C (350°F), Gas Mark 4.

Place the chicken in a roasting tray and lightly oil and heavily season. Roast for an hour and then check that the juices at the thigh bones run clear. You will be serving the chicken at room temperature, so it needs to be very juicy and tender.

Strain the stock and reduce it down again over a high heat until you are left with about 200ml (7fl oz) of liquid. Leave to cool.

To make the *satsivi* sauce, blitz your perfect (or not!) walnuts in a blender or food processor to a powder, then add the garlic, *adjika*, if using, *khmeli-suneli*, confit onions, coriander and cayenne. Pour in most of your stock and blitz to a thin sauce. Keep adding the stock, or water, as needed until you have a double cream-like consistency.

Carve the chicken and place it in a large bowl or a deep platter. In Georgia, they pour the sauce all over and serve the dish at room temperature. With an average toasting session taking a good 15 minutes, no wonder so many Georgian *supra* (see page 172) dishes are served cold!

Tips

The walnuts, whether fresh or dried, need to be the best you can find, flawless with no blemishes, as we are looking for an almost white sauce.

I scatter the dish with some pomegranate seeds in winter or redcurrants if I dare to make it in summer and a few herbs, but that's not traditional.

You can gently heat a little walnut oil and cayenne pepper and drizzle this over the sauce to serve.

Kuchmachi

Do not be scared of the gizzards here. Gizzards... lizards – it's the English word that makes them sound so unappealing. Gizzard is such a harsh term for something so deep and rich in flavour. It was actually the first piece of meat I gave my six-month-old son and he was delighted to "gnaw" on it with his teething-yet-still-toothless mouth. If you are still scared, try this dish using just the hearts. What can be more appealing than eating a being's heart? Especially when it's smothered in ruby, tangy pomegranate sauce and sprinkled with hazelnut shards. This is a dish to be made for an adventurous lover or an anaemic friend. Otherwise, save some of it unsauced and give it to an unsuspecting suffering baby. They would all appreciate it.

Serves 2

3 tablespoons vegetable oil

200g (7oz) chicken hearts, trimmed

200g (7oz) chicken gizzards, trimmed (trimmed weight)

1 large onion, sliced

1 large garlic clove, sliced

30g (1oz) hazelnuts or walnuts, finely chopped

½ teaspoon coriander seeds, toasted and ground

¼ teaspoon cayenne pepper

½ teaspoon dried wild thyme or za'atar herb (optional)

1 teaspoon pomegranate molasses

seeds of ¼ pomegranate

sea salt flakes and freshly ground black pepper

Heat 2 tablespoons of the oil in a frying pan until very hot. Add the hearts and gizzards and leave them to cook for about 2 minutes on each side until caramelized, meaning that it's important not to stir them too often. When a lovely golden crust has formed, take them out of the pan.

Add the remaining tablespoon of oil to the pan and then the onion and cook over a medium-low heat for about 10–15 minutes until softened and started to turn golden. Add the garlic, nuts, spices and herbs and cook for a further 5 minutes.

Return the meat to the pan, add the pomegranate molasses, a splash of water and season well with salt and pepper, then cover with a lid and cook over a low heat for 20–30 minutes until the meat is as soft as you like it (I don't mind it being a tiny bit chewy, so I only cook it for 15 minutes).

Stir through the pomegranate seeds and serve with some rice or bread.

Tips

You can also add some chicken livers – fry them in the pan with everything else, but only add them back in to braise for the last 5 minutes of the cooking time so that they don't become dry and chalky, unless you don't mind dry and chalky, like me, in which case just add them with the hearts and gizzards.

If you have leftovers, this is delicious used as a qutab filling (see page 87).

Watermelon & fish

We have some of the best watermelons in the south of Ukraine, but I never understood why my parents often ate them with big hunks of buttered crusty white bread. Then I went to Lankaran, a city in the southeastern region of Azerbaijan on the Caspian Sea, where my friend Zulya's relatives served us some watermelon with wonderfully flaky salted local fish (*tulum*) and pieces of coarse flatbread for supper, and it all finally made sense to me. The missing link – the salty element – had been found. I was completely won over by the matching of sweet juicy fruit with salty fish and bread. What's not to like! If you can get hold of good-quality salted fish, just eat some watermelon with it, but if you can't, try this more accessible salad. It is a winning combination, trust me. Serve as a starter or an accompaniment to some simple *plov* (see page 128).

Serves 2

10 good-quality anchovy fillets

2 tablespoons good-quality olive oil, plus extra to serve

100g (3½oz) stale sourdough bread, cut into smallish cubes

200g (7oz) watermelon, peeled, deseeded and cut into 5cm (2-inch) cubes

a few very thin slices of red onion

some crunchy lettuce leaves, to serve

Preheat the oven to 180°C (350°F), Gas Mark 4. Using a pestle and mortar, bash the anchovies with the oil into a paste.

Toss the sourdough cubes in the anchovy paste, then spread out on a baking sheet and bake until crispy. Remove from the oven and leave the croûtons to cool.

Gently mix the watermelon, croûtons and onion together and serve with lettuce leaves and an extra drizzle of olive oil.

Chakhapuli

This dish screams spring. A young lamb would be slowly cooked in the tenderest, youngest spring herbs. In Akhaltsikhe in southern Georgia, I've been told this is made outside for a picnic of sorts by the river. The next morning, men would demand to drink the remainder of the juices to cure their sore heads. In Kakheti in eastern Georgia, where the dish is claimed to be from, a local chef told me that this was nonsense because, first of all, there simply wouldn't be any leftovers, he insisted bemused, and secondly, Kakhetian wine is so superior that a hangover is definitely not on the cards. Whatever each region's vibe, this dish is indeed the most delicious ode to spring there is. If you can't find sour plums, add a little verjuice or lemon juice at the end or some good-quality vinegar – I like to add tarragon white wine vinegar to intensify the flavour.

Serves 4–6

2kg (4lb 8oz) very young lean lamb ribs (bone-in) or 1.5kg (3lb 5oz) boneless lamb neck

2 teaspoons coriander seeds, toasted and crushed

2 teaspoons ground blue fenugreek

¼ teaspoon cayenne pepper or 1 teaspoon Red Adjika Salt (see page 62)

350ml (12fl oz) white wine

2 bunches of tarragon, leaves picked and roughly chopped

1 bunch of mint, stalks and all, roughly chopped

1 bunch of coriander, stalks and all, roughly chopped

2 bunches of spring onions, roughly chopped

10 garlic cloves, 8 roughly chopped, 2 crushed

handful of Alycha plums (or greengages), stoned and chopped, or 1 tablespoon verjuice or lemon juice or good-quality wine vinegar

dash of pomegranate molasses (optional)

sea salt flakes

Heat a large, heavy-based flameproof casserole dish. Holding the meat with tongs, cook the pieces, fat side down, over a low-medium heat to render the fat and brown it. If your lamb is fatty, tip the extra fat out.

Add all the spices and cook for a further minute, stirring.

Pour in the wine (and wine vinegar, if using) and let it boil for a minute.

Add half the herbs, all the spring onions and the roughly chopped garlic, season with salt and cover loosely with a lid. Cook for about an hour over a very low heat.

Stir in the sour plums, if available, and cook for 30 minutes–1 hour – you are looking for the meat to be very tender and start to fall off the bone.

When almost ready, add the rest of the herbs and the crushed garlic, along with the verjuice, lemon juice or vinegar if you haven't added the sour plums. Sometimes I also add a dash of pomegranate molasses at this stage. Give it all a good mix, season to taste with salt and serve with some good crusty bread or plain rice.

VARIATION

If stewing lamb is not to your taste, especially if you can't find a young, lean animal, you can do a slow-roast version of this. Simply blitz half the herbs with all the garlic and a couple of preserved lemons in a blender or food processor, mix in the spices and cover a joint of lamb (I'd use a shoulder) in it. Cover with foil and roast in a preheated oven at 160°C (325°F), Gas Mark 3, for 4–5 hours until it is soft and falls apart. Then turn up the oven to 220°C (425°F), Gas Mark 7, remove the foil and roast for a further 10 minutes so that the lamb browns well. Serve with some fresh herbs sprinkled all over it.

Ostriy

The Russian word for "spicy", *ostriy* the dish seems to be a Georgian adaptation of the Russian soup called *solyanka*, "the salty one". It used to be a canteen favourite during Soviet times and it clearly still is. We have seen this dish, and eaten excellent versions of it, in many colourful roadside cafés in Georgia with their gorgeously kitsch oilcloths, small dishes of chilli flakes and funky little salt and pepper shakers. Spicy, rich, salty and with tons of raw onion and coriander, it went perfectly with a cold beer and... a sore head. I really wasn't sure which chapter to put this dish into, but on reflection it should probably have gone in Pain, Be Gone, as this is one of the best things you can eat when feeling tender after a long fun night. You could make it (omitting the gherkins) and freeze it, then pop a portion in the sink to thaw before you go out. The next day, simply add the gherkins when you reheat it and you will be healed!

Serves 6–8

2kg (4lb 8oz) beef ribs or shin

1 bay leaf

4 onions, 3 thickly sliced, 1 thinly sliced

1 tablespoon tomato purée

5 ripe, juicy large tomatoes, coarsely grated, skins discarded

1–3 long red chillies (depending on how hot you like it)

2 teaspoons coriander seeds, lightly toasted and ground

1 teaspoon freshly ground black pepper

1 teaspoon *khmeli-suneli* spice mix

2 Fermented Green Tomatoes (see page 182) or gherkins

3 garlic cloves, crushed

½ bunch of purple or green basil, finely sliced

½ bunch of flat leaf parsley, finely chopped

½ bunch of coriander, leaves picked

sea salt flakes

Put the meat into a large pan and cover with plenty of cold water. Add a little salt and the bay leaf and bring to the boil. Skim off the scum, then reduce the heat to low and cook for 1½ hours until the beef is tender and falling off the bone. Skim off the fat and reserve it for later Remove the meat from the pan, raise the heat and cook the beef stock until reduced by half – you should end up with 500ml (18fl oz) of stock.

Heat the reserved beef fat in a large flameproof casserole dish, add the thickly sliced onions (reserve the thinly sliced onion for serving) and cook them over a medium heat for about 10 minutes until they soften and start taking on some colour. Then add the tomato purée and cook for a further minute over a high heat. Keeping the heat high, add the grated tomatoes and cook for about 10 minutes until reduced and concentrated.

Squash the whole red chillies with the back of your knife and add them to the tomato sauce. Then add all the spices, the meat and the fermented tomatoes or gherkins. This is not a soup but a very saucy stew, so add half a ladleful of the reserved beef stock and then see if it needs a little more.

Cook over a medium-low heat until the stew comes to the boil. Then take it off the heat and add the garlic, basil and parsley. Serve sprinkled with the thinly sliced raw onion and the coriander leaves. Have some beautiful, chunky, soft white bread for mopping up the gravy.

Tip This is supposed to be spicy, but Georgian spicy is not that spicy at all, to be honest. So adjust the heat to your taste by roughly chopping the chillies instead of bruising them, seeds and all, if you wanted it hotter, or make it mild if your family are not hot heads like you and just add some chilli flakes to your portion at the end. Just don't call it ostriy then. Call it nezhniy ("gentle" in Russian).

Tursh kiabab

This is not a kebab as we know it in the West. *Kiabab* in Azerbaijani does indeed mean kebab in English, and in the past the meat for this dish may well have been cooked over fire, but not in this version. And *tursh* simply means "sour". This is slow-cooked herby deliciousness, using the juice from the blitzed-up herbs was a real discovery. So was serving tender slow-cooked meat together with meatballs. And the aubergines here are a gorgeous slippery addition, not unlike snails in the best possible sense. When Zulfiya, who shared this recipe with me, tried snails in a chichi restaurant in Paris in 2004, she closed her eyes and exclaimed, "This tastes exactly like our Lankaran *tursh kiabab!*" Everybody laughed – she had a point. The amount of butter, garlic, parsley and lemon in this beautiful dish is not far off that served with excellent escargots.

Serves 6

2kg (4lb 8oz) leg of mutton on the bone, 700g (1lb 9oz) chopped into cubes, the rest minced – ask your butcher to do this for you

1 onion, roughly chopped

70g (2½oz) flat leaf parsley, plus an extra 200g (7oz)

3 garlic cloves, plus 4 garlic cloves, peeled

150g (5½oz) Clarified Butter (see page 53), plus extra for frying the aubergines

100ml (3½fl oz) verjuice or juice of 2 lemons

dash of white wine vinegar

10 baby aubergines or 2 large

sea salt flakes and freshly ground black pepper

Mix the minced mutton with the onion, the 70g (2½oz) parsley and the 3 garlic cloves, or blitz in a food processor. Cover and chill in the refrigerator for a couple of hours.

Heat 50g (1¾oz) of the Clarified Butter in a cast-iron pan and fry the meat cubes over a high heat until thoroughly caramelized. Add enough water to cover the meat, bring to the boil and skim off the scum, then lower the heat, cover the pan with a lid and cook over a very low heat for about 1 hour until the meat is falling apart. Make sure that the water doesn't evaporate completely, as you will need this stock. Season the meat with salt and pepper and the verjuice or lemon juice.

Blitz the remaining 4 garlic cloves with the 200g (7oz) parsley in a blender or food processor, then squeeze out the juice, but don't throw it away. Mix half the blitzed herb mixture with the mince mixture, and season well with salt and pepper.

Heat the remaining 100g (3½oz) Clarified Butter in a large pan and fry the rest of the blitzed parsley and garlic until the herbs are dry but not burnt.

Mix the vinegar and some salt into a bowl of water and use to wet your hands before you shape the mince mixture into marble-sized meatballs (wetting your hands makes this easier), then place in the refrigerator.

If using baby aubergines, fry them whole in a little Clarified Butter until golden all over. If using large aubergines, slice them into 2cm (¾-inch) rounds before frying.

Add the fried parsley and garlic to the lamb stock and bring it to the boil, then very gently drop the meatballs into stock. Now add the herb juice, lower the heat to its minimum, cover with a lid and cook for 30 minutes.

Add the aubergines to the pan, check for seasoning and cook for a further 15 minutes. Serve with Shakh Plov (see page 128) and natural yogurt or Homemade Matsoni (see page 29).

VARIATION
You can use a few tablespoons of vegetable oil instead of the Clarified Butter for cooking the blitzed parsley and garlic, but the flavour will be different.

Mtsvadi

The secret of beautiful Kakhetian barbecued pork is to use the highest-quality meat and cook it over grape vine coals very slowly. The meat is not usually seasoned until it is cooked. Kakhetian rare-breed pigs roam the hills feeding themselves on the land. Georgians in general prefer breeding animals that can take care of themselves and feed on wild plants growing around them. While you are sourcing the best-possible meat for this dish, ask a friend with an allotment if there are any grape vines around. I have and as a consequence I can now make this authentic Georgian dish in London in the summer! Failing that, try finding some fruit tree chips to use for your barbecue to replicate at least a tiny bit of the pork's beauty – they will make a big difference to the flavour of the meat.

Serves 4

800g (1lb 12oz) pork fillet or neck fillet (which I prefer, as it has more fat), chopped into large chunks

red or white wine, for basting

2 Turkish flatbreads (or any good-quality flatbreads you can easily find)

fine sea salt

TO GARNISH

2 mild onions, thinly sliced and soaked in iced water to reduce the harshness

1 pomegranate, half juiced and half seeds kept intact

handful of coriander leaves

You will also need 2 (preferably) massive metal skewers, a large quantity of dry vine twigs (or fruit tree kindling) and a barbecue

Thread the pork on to your metal skewers.

Take a big bunch of dry vine twigs and light them, making sure you keep some in reserve in case the fire dies down and you need to feed it. They will burn very quickly and fiercely, and will produce quite a bit of smoke, so warn your neighbours if you are doing this in the city. Let the twigs burn right down into coals. The meat should be quite close to the coals, and the coals glowing intensely. If they should start burning when the meat is over them, douse the fire with a little water.

Meanwhile, mix some salt into the red or white wine for basting, 2 tablespoons salt to 1 litre (1¾ pints) wine.

Cook the skewers over the vine embers, turning every so often and basting with the salted wine from time to time. This can take up to 20 minutes. The meat will be caramelized at the edges but still extremely juicy and soft inside. Check one after 15 minutes to see if it is cooked.

Now the best part. Grab one of the breads and, working over a large bowl, use it to slide the meat off one of the skewers and into the bowl. Then add the bread to the bowl and use the other bread to slide off the rest of the meat. If you have cooked the meat properly, it will still be so juicy that the best part of the meal will be the meat-juice-soaked bread.

Drain the onions well and season them with salt. Pour the pomegranate juice over them, sprinkle with the coriander and pomegranate seeds and serve with the meat, along with some chopped garden vegetables.

Zahir's stoned chicken

Chef Zahir is one of the most friendly yet serious chefs I have ever met. He has worked at Xanlar, a restaurant in the city of Qebele in Azerbaijan, since he was 14 years old. Zahir's boss was determined to re-create a truly ancient method of cooking meat, whereby two heavy stones were heated and a piece of meat or vegetables with essential *kurdyuk* fat (see page 232) were squashed between the stones, so he built a special stove that makes the technique possible. Fired by wood at the base, a huge slab of limestone is heated to the maximum, with another piece of limestone placed on top. We were getting impatient at the thought of chicken and vegetables pressed against each other cooking in young lamb fat. It all felt so primordially delicious.

Re-creating this approach at home is more of a challenge, but it's not impossible. If lamb fat is not your thing or you can't find the good stuff, try lard or *lardo* (Italian cured pigs' fat). Chicken will never have tasted so good.

Serves 2–4

50g (1¾oz) lamb fat (or use lard, *lardo* or a thick piece of pancetta)

2 green chillies, left whole

1 green pepper, cored, deseeded and sliced into large chunks

3 medium potatoes, unpeeled and sliced into thin rounds

1 medium aubergine, sliced into 1cm (½-inch) rounds

2 poussins or 1 small organic chicken

2 flavoursome tomatoes, sliced on the equator (optional)

2 flatbreads

sea salt flakes and freshly ground black pepper

You will also need 2 roasting trays, one slightly larger than the other, and a heavy weight such as 2 bricks wrapped in foil or a heavy, heat-resistant pestle and mortar

Preheat the oven to 220°C (425°F), Gas Mark 7. Place the oven shelf at the very bottom of the oven, and remove all the other shelves, as you need space to put your weight on top.

When all the vegetables are prepped, spatchcock your poussins or chicken. Place the bird breast side down on a chopping board, and, using sharp kitchen scissors or a knife, cut along either side of the backbone. Then turn the bird over and flatten with the palm of your hand.

Heat the animal fat in the larger roasting tray in the oven until sizzling. Heat the other smaller roasting tray and your heavy weight at the same time.

Carefully add the poussins or chicken cut side down on top of the fat in the larger tray and layer the vegetables all around (except the tomatoes). Cover everything with greaseproof paper and top with the smaller tray.

Put the whole thing into your super-hot oven and place the hot weight on top of the smaller tray, then roast for 40 minutes for the poussin, or about an hour if you are using a chicken, adding the tomatoes 7 minutes before the end of the cooking time, if using.

Remove the weight, small tray and paper, then tuck the flatbreads underneath the chicken and cook for a further 5 minutes. Check that the chicken is done by pulling at one of the legs – it should pull away easily and the juices should run clear.

I like to serve everything on a platter, with a little natural yogurt, whole bunches of herbs and whole radishes and maybe a squeeze of lemon juice.

Tip *If I can find them, I would always substitute Spanish Padrón peppers for the green pepper and chillies in this recipe, as they work so well here and you might get a surprise spicy kick.*

Lyulya kebabs

Making these kebabs requires a little skill and some culinary sensitivity. The first time I tried an incredible *lyulya* kebab was in the Syrian Club, a restaurant in Cyprus, and I could never find its match. That was until I tried the recipe of one of the most prominent modern cookbook authors and Central Asia experts, Stalik Khankishiev, whose creative and fun descriptions are teaching new generations of amateurs and curious chefs alike brilliant regional techniques, including how to grill meat properly. This is his method and I swear by it. Using good-quality meat is important and you need to include extra fat. It's vital not to lose the meat's succulence by using machines to chop up the meat but to use your hands instead. You must also make sure that you massage the minced meat mixture properly for the proteins to bind the meat, and then chill it. He gives so much detailed advice. Turn this into a fun project and devote an hour to it, and you will have the juiciest of kebabs.

Makes approx. 13 skewers, enough for a small crowd

1.5kg (3lb 5oz) boneless, fatty lamb (such as neck), cut into 4 large chunks

250g (9oz) lamb fat (ask your butcher)

250g (9oz) onion, very finely diced

2 teaspoons freshly ground black pepper

2 teaspoons ground cumin

2 teaspoons ground coriander

2 tablespoons sea salt flakes

TO SERVE

flatbreads

sliced onion

pomegranate seeds

You will also need 2 heavy meat cleavers, 10 large metal skewers, preferably self-rotating, and a barbecue

You will need to hand-mince the meat. This is a recipe for the perfect kebab, so there is no other way but to do it by hand. Work on a large wooden chopping board, ideally on a table that is not too high so that you only need to drop your hand with the cleaver without having to bring it up again – it's hard work! So, take your 2 meat cleavers and then, looking to find a rhythm, start dropping the cleavers, one at a time, into the meat. If the meat sticks to the blades, wash them in hot water. You can also rub them with fat so that the meat doesn't stick as much.

When the meat has been minced, chop up the fat and mix it into the meat in a large bowl, then add the onions. Add the spices to the meat mixture and mix again, really working it with your hands, as the more you do, the firmer the kebabs will cling to the metal skewer.

Once the meat mixture has been well worked, cover the bowl with clingfilm and place in the refrigerator for at least 30 minutes so that the fat cools down and works as a binding agent when the kebabs are shaped.

Light your barbecue and let it burn down.

Have a bowl of warm water ready on your work surface for you to wet your hands while shaping the meat mixture. Take 150g (5½oz) of the meat mixture, enough for 1 kebab, and shape it into a tight sphere. It should look solid and not have any cracks.

Pierce the sphere with a large metal skewer. Using your hand, squeeze the sphere and gently distribute it along the length of the skewer. Keep wetting your hand in a bowl of water to help the process along and prevent the meat from sticking to your hands. Finally, make sure that you really pinch the meat mixture at either end of the skewer so that it's firmly stuck to the skewer.

The cooking process should ideally be done on a barbecue that has self-rotating skewers since, for best results, they need to be turned constantly over mildly glowing hot coals. This way, the kebabs will develop an even golden crust and they will be very juicy. But if you don't have the kit, keep turning the skewers every few minutes for about 10 minutes until evenly cooked. Serve the juicy kebabs over flatbreads on a platter with a little sliced onion and pomegranate seeds.

Fish with pistachio & cauliflower sauce & kindzmari

This dish came out of the numerous Georgian supper clubs I have staged in the UK. I love the creaminess of Georgian nut sauces like *satsivi* (see pages 136–7), but also the acidity and aroma of *kindzmari*, so this is a great way to enjoy a bit of both. If you are cooking for a dinner party and want to dress it up in style, you can also add something crispy on top as I've suggested below. If you want to simplify the recipe, simply drop one of the sauces – a good fish would be equally delicious with either a dollop of the nutty cauliflower mixture or a slick of *kindzmari* and some simple boiled potatoes, depending on whether your preference is for creamy comfort or a spicy kick. But if you do have the time and the will, this is not a difficult dish to prepare, especially if you aim to impress someone.

Serves 4

2 tablespoons vegetable oil

4 hake fillets

PISTACHIO & CAULIFLOWER SAUCE

½ small cauliflower, divided into florets

2 shallots, peeled and halved

25g (1oz) unsalted butter

200ml (⅓ pint) warm chicken, fish or vegetable stock

small pinch of saffron threads

70g (2½oz) pistachios or walnuts, toasted

sea salt flakes and freshly ground black pepper

KINDZMARI

25g (1oz) bunch of coriander, stalks and all, roughly chopped

2 green chillies, roughly chopped

1 garlic clove, roughly chopped

2 tablespoons white wine vinegar

1 tablespoon maple syrup or clear honey

sea salt flakes, to taste

TO SERVE (IF YOU WANT TO BE FANCY)

floured and shallow-fried shallot rings (or toasted flaked almonds or crispy seaweed)

herbs or micro leaves

pomegranate seeds

To make the pistachio & cauliflower sauce, preheat the oven to 180°C (350°F), Gas Mark 4. Pop the cauliflower florets and halved shallots on to a baking tray, dot around the butter and pour over half the chicken stock. Season well with salt. Crush the saffron with a little sea salt using a pestle and mortar and add that as well.

Roast the vegetables for about 30 minutes until the liquid has gone and they look soft and caramelized. If the cauliflower catches a little bit at the edges, it's not a problem, and the same applies to the shallots – you need them to have colour for the sauce to be flavoursome.

continued »

Grind the pistachios in a powerful food processor (or use an electric spice or coffee grinder) into a powder. Then blitz the shallots and cauliflower with the ground nuts in a blender or food processor until the mixture is super smooth, adding some more of the warm stock if the mixture needs help to blend. It should be the consistency of double cream, but if your blender or processor is not strong enough to produce a completely smooth sauce, don't worry – it will still taste good. Taste and season some more if you feel that it's still under-seasoned.

To make the *kindzmari* sauce, blitz all the ingredients in (again!) a powerful blender or food processor. The resulting mixture should be quite liquid but smooth, without any bits of stalk, and the flavour should be primarily sour but also spicy and a tiny bit sweet. You can drop the maple syrup or honey for a more authentically tart version, but I like the hint of sweetness here. The sauce may turn a dark, muddy green, but who cares as long as it's delicious!

To cook the hake, preheat the oven to 200°C (400°F), Gas Mark 6.

Heat the oil in a large frying pan with an ovenproof handle. Season the fish skin with salt and pop it down into the hot oil. After a minute, shake the pan gently so that the skin doesn't get stuck. Cook for 2 minutes, then flip the fish over and transfer the pan to the oven for a further 5–7 minutes (depending on the thickness of your fillet) to finish cooking it.

To serve the fancy way, put some slightly warmed cauliflower sauce on a plate, dot around a spoonful of *kindzmari* and then add the hot fish skin side up. Scatter over the shallots or almonds, seaweed, herbs or pomegranate seed garnish, if using.

VARIATIONS

I've used pistachios here because I love them, although walnuts would be more traditional, but I don't see a problem with using any nut you fancy and I struggle to find good walnuts in UK – just use the best you can get hold of. Quality is what's important here.

A piece of expertly cooked pork fillet would not be out of place here instead of the fish. I have also made this using scallops, or if you want to go vegetarian, fry a cauliflower steak in some butter and a little oil until caramelized.

Fish lavangi

In the West, we are constantly told that meat must be really tender – heaven forbid that there is any resistance to the teeth or any cartilage! We are also told that fish must only see the pan for a fleeting moment, otherwise it will become dry and inedible. In many cases, yes indeed, braised meat is nicer if falling apart, or a steak if expertly cooked or fish if quickly roasted until it is only just cooked. But there is also room for slightly chewy gizzards, or slow-cooked liver that is no longer pink or slightly chewy pork *mtsvadi*. We have teeth for a reason and not everything needs to melt in the mouth. In Lankaran in southeastern Azerbaijan, they love to cook fish slowly in a *tandyr* or outside clay oven, stuffed with a delicious juicy filling. Some may think that the flesh is a little drier than what is usually considered desirable, but I love how crispy the skin gets and I am fine with the texture of the fish, so I have not adapted this recipe to the Western palate. The stuffing has time to cook properly inside the fish, developing and exchanging flavours with its flesh. It is absolutely delicious and I urge you try it, especially in winter when walnuts are of the best quality. Not everyone has a *tandyr* oven in their backyard or garden, not even in Lankaran, so a frying pan and a lid are used, but you can also use the oven.

Serves 2

1 whole sea bream, about 700g (1lb 9oz), gutted and scaled

4 tablespoons Alycha paste (*tursha*) or soaked sour fruit leather (*lavashana*) or tamarind paste

2 tablespoons plain flour, if frying

corn oil, if frying

sea salt flakes and freshly ground black pepper

Summer filling

handful of dried Alycha plums or dried sour cherries

2 red onions, peeled and finely chopped

1 green pepper, cored, deseeded and finely chopped

1 red chilli, finely chopped

½ bunch of mint, leaves picked and finely chopped

½ bunch of flat leaf parsley, leaves picked and finely chopped

½ bunch of coriander, leaves picked and finely chopped

½ bunch of purple basil, leaves picked and finely chopped

2 tomatoes, finely chopped

grated zest and juice of 1 lemon

You will also need a large, stout needle and thread

continued »

For the filling, soak the dried Alycha plums or sour cherries in some warm water for an hour until they become plump.

Drain the dried fruit, then mix with the rest of the filling ingredients, seasoning well with salt and pepper, getting in there with your hands and massaging the ingredients together really well.

Slash the fish along the backbone and then rub with some salt and pepper and the Alycha paste or *lavashana* or tamarind paste all over the fish's skin.

Stuff the filling into the belly of the fish – it has to be pretty full and bulging – then grab your needle and thread and sew up the belly to enclose the filling.

Dust one side of the fish with the flour.

Heat some corn oil in a large frying pan over a medium heat and fry the fish on the floured side for 2 minutes. Flip the fish, then cover the pan with a lid, lower the heat and cook for about 30–40 minutes until the skin is well browned. Serve with some rice or Saffron Plov (see page 120) with some cooked lentils stirred through.

Winter filling

400g (14oz) banana shallots, peeled

100g (3½oz) walnuts, lightly toasted and ground into a powder

3 tablespoons Alycha paste (*tursha*) or handful of dried Alycha plums or blitzed dried sour cherries or tamarind paste

sea salt flakes and freshly ground black pepper

You will also need a piece of muslin

Blitz the shallots in a blender or food processor, then enclose in the muslin and squeeze out all the juice. You will end up with a handful of wrung-out shallot.

Mix the shallots with 2 tablespoons of the Alycha paste and all the other ingredients, seasoning well with salt and pepper. You can freeze this mixture at this point for up to a month.

Preheat the oven to 180°C (350°F), Gas Mark 4.

Prepare the fish as in the main recipe above, rubbing the remaining Alycha paste or *lavashana* inside the belly of the fish as well as over the skin.

Stuff the fish with the filling mixture as in the main recipe above.

Place the fish on a baking tray and roast in the oven for 30–40 minutes.

Tip In Azerbaijan, they use kutum or Caspian roach for this dish, a predator that feeds on crustaceans, so just imagine the resulting flavour of the fish! I have suggested sea bream as a more widely available option, or you can try red mullet instead, but feel free to choose the best sustainable fish you can find.

Boy, do they know how to drink in Georgia. A *tamada*, or toast master, can easily kill 12 litres (25 pints) of wine during a *supra*, a Georgian feast. Every toast (which is more of a poetical philosophical discussion) takes at least 15 minutes, so there are long pauses. Pauses or none, it depends on how good the wine is. It isn't always perfect, so the next day a cure is needed, and Georgians know the best cures in Caucasus. Initially, I thought this would be the "hangover chapter", but actually this is a chapter for those who need nourishment. The broths here will cure a grown man's sore head as well as help a small child recover from a cold equally well.

pain, be gone!

Village breakfast

We often make a breakfast like this in Ukraine (it's my Aunt Lynda's speciality), and this is what I cooked up in Tbilisi for friends, which they loved, spiced up with a little chilli. After all, Georgians are the great recipe adaptors (see *Ostriy*, page 144). It's a perfect dish for using up old bread, and although it's called breakfast, it also makes a great lunch or dinner – in fact, this is my universal, go-to meal. The ingredients always include cured pork fat, bread, eggs and tomatoes, but the rest depends on what I have in the refrigerator; dill and green chillies often figure. This is simply one of the best meals in the world.

Serves 2

1 large ripe tomato

2 garlic cloves, crushed with salt

20g (¾oz) *lardo*, torn if in thin slices or finely chopped

4 small pieces of stale bread (sourdough, rye or anything you like)

1 red or green chilli, diced

4 eggs

½ tablespoon chopped dill

½ tablespoon chopped coriander

½ tablespoon chopped basil

sea salt flakes

Slice the tomato across the equator into 4 rounds and spread a tiny smidgen of the crushed garlic over them.

Heat the *lardo* in a large frying pan over a medium heat, and when it starts to melt and sizzle, add the bread. Cook on one side until it starts to soften, then flip the bread pieces over and cook for another minute. Prop the bread up against the insides of the pan to make room for the rest of the ingredients.

Add the tomato rounds to the pan, garlic side up, and throw in the chilli. Make a little space for the eggs and crack them all around the bread and tomato rounds.

Cook for about 5–7 minutes or until the whites are set but the yolks are still runny. Sprinkle a little salt over the egg yolks, throw over the chopped herbs and serve immediately.

Tomato scramble

I love egg yolks. Even though they are healthier for you, I never finish eating the white of a fried egg – too rubbery, too bland. I do love scrambled eggs, though, and in particular the combination of scrambled egg and sweet tomato. They do this in Azerbaijan a lot, including my friend Zulya who leaves the egg yolks whole! When I heard this, I knew it would be my favourite scrambled egg dish. So here is the perfect version – egg whites scrambled with tomato, with the egg yolks remaining whole and glorious, ready for your bread! Serve this dish as part of a bigger feast.

Serves 2

30g (1oz) unsalted butter

2 garlic cloves, grated

3 ripe, tasty tomatoes, grated (see Tip below)

a little granulated sugar, to taste, if needed

4 eggs

1 tablespoon chopped coriander or any other soft herb, such as dill (optional)

sea salt flakes

sourdough bread, to serve

Melt the butter in a frying pan, add the garlic and cook over a low heat, stirring from time to time, for about 3–5 minutes or until the garlic starts smelling sweet. Be careful not to burn it.

Stir in the tomato pulp and then season the mixture with salt. Taste it and add a little sugar if you think it needs it. Cook the tomatoes for about 5–10 minutes until reduced and quite dry.

Now the fun part begins. Crack the 4 eggs into the pan and gently mix the whites into the tomato sauce, scrambling them, leaving the egg yolks intact. Keep scrambling the whites with the tomatoes gently over a low heat until they have set to your liking and the yolks look sufficiently heated through.

Sprinkle some sea salt over the yolks and add the herbs, if using, then eat, squashing the egg yolks into some sourdough bread and wiping the plate clean with the bread at the end.

Tip Slice the tomato in half and grate it over a coarse box grater. If the tomato is decent (I wouldn't recommend using anything else), don't throw away the skin but chop it finely and add it, too.

Khash

Stop gawping. This has nothing to do with charas or hashish, although its taste is as beautifully intoxicating. *Khash* is the ultimate hangover cure – a deeply meaty, thick broth, so simple, so genius. Pretty much every country in the Caucasus claims a right to its invention, but the point is, it doesn't really matter where it originated. I once had something very similar cooked for me by a Colombian friend's mum (called *caldo de costilla*, I believe), so this kind of dish is probably universal. I like the story of its origins in Georgia as a hangover cure – after a long, heavy night of feasting and drinking, a few large pieces of beef (and often some tripe) would be thrown into the pot before going to bed and cooked slowly all night. In the early hours, woken by a throbbing headache, the men would get up, pour a bowl of the viscous, sweet broth, add some salt and garlic, eat it, go back to bed and wake up again fresh as the morning dew… probably only to go and enjoy another day of partying. Nowadays, people visit *khasherias*, eateries that specialize in *khash*. I must constantly remind myself to explain what those places actually are when back in the West, as eyes widen awkwardly when I mention the word!

Serves 6

2kg (4lb 8oz) good-quality beef shin or ribs

500g (1lb 2oz) tripe – order in advance from your butcher and ask them to prep it for you (optional)

2 onions, peeled but left whole

2 fresh bay leaves, crumbled

TO SERVE

3 tablespoons chopped coriander

3 tablespoons chopped dill

3 tablespoons chopped purple or green basil

10 garlic cloves, finely grated

sea salt flakes

freshly ground black pepper or chilli flakes (optional)

Put the meat into a large pan, cover with cold water and add the onions and bay, then bring to the boil over a medium heat. Skim off the foam that forms just as the broth is about to boil, then reduce the heat to its lowest setting.

Cook the meat for a few hours until it is very tender and starts falling apart, adding a little water to the pan if it reduces too much, and remember to keep skimming off the scum.

When the stock is strong and the meat is tender, it is time to serve it. Put the herbs, garlic and salt into separate small *pialas* (small ceramic bowls) and encourage your hungover guests to help themselves and season the broth to their liking. Feel free to add plenty of freshly ground black pepper or chilli flakes.

Poputsa's chikhirtma

Georgian men often name their daughters after the women who meant a lot to them. Nino's grandmother's real name was Ketevan, but Nino only knew her as Poputsa, a name that Nino's great grandfather gave his little girl after his ex-beloved who was also a famous Georgian writer. Before we took the photograph for this recipe (see pages 174–5), we were shown a lot of Poputsa's remarkable dowry – a rug she'd woven herself, an early 20th-century tea set and a stunning 19th-century Kuznetsov "dinner set". When Georgians have a *supra*, an elaborate, often all-night feast with much drinking and many a philosophical toast, the guests sometimes continue into the early hours with a morning *supra* – an after-party. If a hangover is already setting in, then *chikhirtma* is the soup of choice for some. It consists of a rich chicken stock, thickened with toasted flour and egg and spiked with vinegar, so rich and sharp at the same time. Served with a shot of *chacha* (Georgian grappa), this dish is eaten before going off to bed to slumber, only to wake up a few hours later refreshed and ready to repeat the feasting, especially if it's a special occasion like a wedding or a funeral.

Serves 6–8

1kg (2lb 4oz) boiling chicken or 2 organic chicken carcasses

1 onion, peeled but left whole

2 carrots, scrubbed and roughly chopped

2 celery sticks, roughly chopped

5 black peppercorns

2 shallots, diced

1 tablespoon plain flour

1 bunch of coriander, leaves separated, stalks and roots (if the latter are available, well washed) chopped

pinch of saffron threads

3 egg yolks

2 tablespoons white wine vinegar

sea salt flakes

Place the chicken or chicken carcasses, onion, carrots, celery, peppercorns and a pinch of salt in a 3-litre (5¼-pint) pan of cold water. Bring to the boil, then skim off the foam and lower the heat. Cook for an hour or until the chicken is tender and the liquid has reduced by one-third.

Skim 2–3 tablespoons of the chicken fat off the surface of the broth and pour it into a frying pan. Heat the fat, add the shallots and cook gently for 5–10 minutes until starting to caramelize ever so slightly, if you have the patience. Keep adding more skimmed chicken fat if the pan becomes too dry – it should have some moisture before adding the flour.

Add the flour and a touch more chicken fat and cook, stirring, for a few minutes to cook out the flour. Then add the coriander stalks and roots and cook for about 5 minutes to soften.

Lift the chicken out of the broth and shred the meat into pieces – if you wish; it will make it easier to eat later.

Add the shallot and coriander mixture to the broth. Grind the saffron with a little salt using a pestle and mortar, stir in a dash of the broth and then pour the saffron liquid into the broth.

Whisk the egg yolks and vinegar together, then whisk into the gently simmering broth. Add the shredded chicken meat and cook for a few minutes, then serve scattered with the chopped coriander leaves.

We accidentally spilled some wine at Nino's mum's place, meaning that her ancestors had given her the green light and welcomed us into their home.

Tarragon soup

Keti Sujashvili from Kazbegi in northeastern Georgia gave me this soup on a rainy June afternoon and I fell in love with it. When she told me the recipe, I knew it would be one of my very favourite in the entire book. It is so easy to make and won't take you longer than 30 minutes, but it packs a real punch of flavour. Once when I cooked this I forgot to add the rice and I didn't miss it, but do add it if you prefer thicker soups. If you use the eggs, they will add body to the soup, but only add the egg if you're intending to eat it all on the day of cooking.

Serves 6

50g (1¾oz) unsalted butter

2 potatoes, peeled and roughly chopped

2 litres (3½ pints) water

2 tablespoons mild olive oil

1 onion, diced

2 carrots, scrubbed and coarsely grated

1 green pepper, cored, deseeded and sliced

1 red pepper, cored, deseeded and sliced

2 large ripe tomatoes, grated (see Tip on page 167), skin discarded

70g (2½oz) basmati rice (optional)

generous pinch of chilli flakes

2 eggs, lightly beaten (optional)

2 small garlic cloves, finely grated

1 bunch of tarragon, leaves picked and chopped

sea salt flakes

Heat the butter in a saucepan, add the potatoes and coat them in the butter, then add the measured water and a generous pinch of salt. Cook over a low heat for about 5 minutes.

Heat the oil in a frying pan, add the onion and cook for about 7 minutes until soft and starting to go golden, then add the carrots and cook for about 3 minutes until they also start getting a little colour, too.

Finally, add the peppers and sauté for a few minutes, then add the tomatoes. Keep stirring from time to time, so as not to let the mixture burn.

Add the sautéed vegetables, and the rice if using, to the potatoes and stock and cook for 10 minutes or until the rice and potatoes are tender.

Lower the heat so that the stock is barely bubbling, add the chilli flakes and then gradually add the eggs, if using, whisking them in thoroughly.

Finally, whisk in the garlic, add the tarragon and take the soup off the hob to serve.

Golnar's herb stalk broth

Ways of incorporating one's culture into a completely different environment can be really ingenious. Golnar, who was born in Germany but has grown up listening to her Azerbaijani grandmother's stories without ever having visited her homeland, had one of the strongest cultural and culinary longings I have ever seen in a person. The flavours of Azerbaijan and Persia are in her Berlin kitchen everywhere you look – spices, butter, dried fruit and of course herbs. Fresh herbs, whole bunches of tarragon, dill, coriander, wild garlic and basil adorning the table, making almost a dish in themselves. In the morning, she took out a pot of incredibly flavoursome herb stock made from a bunch of herb stalks. The meatballs were rustled up in a few minutes, and some garlic and chopped dandelion (common in Berlin in April) added to the broth at the end. It was one of the most delicious breakfasts I've had in a long time. Any bitter crunchy vegetable will do if cultivated dandelion is not common where you live. I have tried this with roughly chopped chicory and Swiss chard, but absolutely anything will work.

Serves 4–6

300g (10½oz) aromatic herb stalks, such as tarragon, coriander, basil and flat leaf parsley, gently bruised (reserve some of the leaves for chopping to serve)

2 litres (3½ pints) cold water

4 garlic cloves, 2 sliced, 2 crushed

200g (7oz) minced beef or lamb

small handful of dill

small handful of tarragon

2 tablespoons pomegranate molasses

3 dandelion stalks (or celery sticks, chicory or Swiss chard), roughly chopped

sea salt flakes

Put the whole stalks into the cold water in a large pan, add the sliced garlic and some salt and bring to the boil. Lower the heat and simmer for about 10 minutes. If you have time, leave the broth to cool and further infuse with the herb flavour. Strain the stalks out, but keep the stock.

Put the minced meat, some salt and the dill and tarragon in a blender or food processor and blitz until well combined. Using slightly wet hands, form the meat mixture into small meatballs, about 1cm (½ inch).

Bring the stock to the boil, add the meatballs and the pomegranate molasses and cook for 5–8 minutes until the meatballs are tender and cooked through.

Finally, add the crushed garlic and dandelion stalks (or whatever crunchy stalks you have available) and cook for a further 2 minutes – you want them to remain fresh and still a little crunchy. Serve with a warm hunk of bread and the reserved chopped herb leaves.

Fermented jonjoli

Hallelujah! You can now get jonjoli (ready-fermented) online (see page 234)! Jonjoli. It is gorgeous and it exists. But here is what you do should you come across some of the beautiful fresh clusters of white flower buds – or if you decide to move to Georgia! I hear it can be found in Italy and the Balkans too, although I always thought it was endemic to Georgia. Or try using the flower buds of the pseudoacacia tree if you can find some in your area (see page 228). They say to avoid washing the buds and to pick them after a spring rain (very romantic!).

Makes a 500g (1lb 2oz) jar
  2kg (4lb 8oz) jonjoli flower bud clusters, shaken free of any insects
  40g (1½oz) sea salt flakes

  You will also need a sterilized 500g (1lb 2oz) preserving jar, muslin pressed
  with a hot iron to sterilize it and a small ceramic or glass dish or jar that will
  fit inside the neck of the preserving jar

Pack the jonjoli into a sterilized preserving jar, adding salt between the layers and pressing down with your hands.

Cover the top of the jar with a piece of the muslin, then insert a small dish or something heavy to weight down the jonjoli.

Leave it in your kitchen for a week or two (depending on temperature) to start the fermentation process, cleaning and changing the muslin every day.

Remove the muslin and weight, seal the jar and pop it in the refrigerator. It should keep for a few months. You may need to rinse it before serving if it tastes too salty.

Pickled green chillies

Pickling and fermenting is the way of life in Georgia. Pickles come out in winter as often as they do in summer. From gorgeous and unique jonjoli (bladdernut) buds and fermented green tomatoes to these beautiful chillies, they stimulate the appetite and cut through the saltiness of dishes they are often served with.

Makes a 1.4-litre (2½-pint) jar
   1.5kg (3lb 5oz) long green chillies
   1 litre (1¾ pints) natural spring or still mineral water
   15g (½oz) fine sea salt
   25ml (2 tablespoons) white wine vinegar or other good-quality mild vinegar
   washed maize or sweetcorn leaves (see Tip below) or washed green parts of leeks or sturdy cabbage leaves

   You will also need a sterilized 1.4-litre (2½-pint) preserving jar and muslin pressed with a hot iron to sterilize it

First we need to prep the chillies. This is a curious (for me) way of prepping and preserving chillies, but this is the recipe Nino gave me, and I am going with it. Leave your chillies out in your kitchen for a day so that they become a little softer.

On the second day, cut off the stalks of the chillies and leave them out for another day.

Wash the chillies and drain them in a colander, then pack them tightly into the sterilized jar.

Put the water into a pan, add the salt and heat gently, stirring, until dissolved, then leave to cool completely. Mix the cooled brine with the vinegar and pour it over the chillies.

Cover the jar with a piece of muslin and leave in your kitchen for about 3 days, cleaning and changing the muslin every day.

Removing the muslin, Nino then covers the chillies with the maize or sweetcorn leaves, which she says tint the chillies a lovely golden colour and absorb some of the extra spice. If you can't find these leaves, I often use the green parts of leeks or some sturdy cabbage leaves. Seal the jar and store in a cool, dark place for up to a couple of months.

Tip Look for sweetcorn cobs still in their wrapping of leaves at markets or greengrocers in late summer into autumn.

Fermented green tomatoes

These are truly mind-blowing, delivering the strongest umami and chilli kick you can imagine. You can eat them as they are or chop them finely and serve with oysters. Or use them to make a delicious relish to go with grilled meat or serve with some buttery, milky mashed potatoes. In fact, if you are hungover, ask your loved one to make you some luscious mash, then eat just that, gentle and creamy potatoes that don't require you to even chew, along with these tomatoes, so savoury and sour, salty and firm.

Makes 3 x 1-litre (1¾-pint) jars
  3 litres (5¼ pints) natural spring or still mineral water
  40g (1½oz) fine sea salt
  1 teaspoon allspice berries
  10 black peppercorns
  1 fresh bay leaf, crushed
  2kg (4lb 8oz) green or other firm tomatoes

  2 long red chillies, sliced
  5 garlic cloves, sliced
  4 celery sticks with leaves, leaves separated and stalks chopped

  You will also need a 5.5 litre (8-pint) sterilized preserving jars muslin pressed with a hot iron to sterilize it and a ceramic or glass dish or jar that will fit inside the neck of the preserving jar

Put the water into a large pan, add the salt and heat gently, stirring, until dissolved. Add the allspice berries, peppercorns and bay and bring to the boil, then leave to cool completely.

Meanwhile, make 2 slashes in the form of a cross in the base of each tomato. Stuff each tomato where you have slashed it with 1–2 slices of chilli and garlic and some celery leaves.

Put some of the chopped celery sticks into the base of the sterilized preserving jar, then pack the stuffed tomatoes on top. Add some more celery to the very top of the jar (place some long stalks across the top to keep the tomatoes submerged) and pour over the brine. Cover the top of the jar with a piece of the muslin, then insert a small dish or jar partially filled with water into the top of the jar to weight down the ingredients and keep them submerged.

Leave the jar in the kitchen to ferment for 4–10 days, depending on how warm the environment is – the warmer, the quicker they will ferment. Clean and change the muslin every day. If you see mould appearing, do not panic – just remove it carefully with a spoon. You are looking for the water to start bubbling and for the tomatoes to soften and go slightly fizzy. Once they are pleasantly fizzy and sour, store the jar in the refrigerator or in a cellar or other cold place to slow down the fermentation process. They should keep for up to 2 months. If the brine turns slimy, unfortunately it's game over.

Fermented beetroot & cauliflower

This is another recipe from my Armenian relatives, although beetroot is of course used to colour and flavour pickles all over the Caucasus and the Middle East. There is something very special about coupling it with cauliflower. The textures, the colour, the flavour; everything sings. I urge you to make this one – winter will never have felt this vibrant. And do experiment with flavourings, such as adding a few sprigs of hard herbs, such as thyme, or pink peppercorns. This is not the traditional approach, but flavours like ginger, orange and cumin and coriander seeds would also be welcome additions here.

Makes a 3-litre (5¼-pint) jar

1 litre (1¾ pints) natural spring or still mineral water

25g (1oz) fine sea salt

10 allspice berries

2 bay leaves

4 beetroots

1 cauliflower (I use Romanseco)

15 garlic cloves, separated and unpeeled

stick of celery

You will also need a sterilized 3-litre (5¼-pint) preserving jar and muslin pressed with a hot iron to sterilize it

Put the water into a large pan, add the salt and heat gently, stirring, until dissolved. Add the allspice and bay (or whatever aromatics you choose) and bring to the boil, then leave to cool completely.

Peel the beetroots and slice into thin wedges. Separate the cauliflower into florets, slicing in half if large, and chop the stalk. Pack the vegetables into your sterilized jar.

Pour the cooled brine and aromatics over the beetroot and cauliflower. Make sure the vegetables are fully submerged in the brine – I wedge a stick of celery across the neck of the jar to hold everything else down.

Cover the jar with a piece of the muslin and leave in your kitchen for about 5 days, cleaning and changing the muslin every day. The timing really depends on how warm your kitchen is, but you are looking for bubbles and for the vegetables to soften slightly but still be firm and pleasantly sour. Once ready, remove the celery and muslin, seal the jar and keep in a cool, dark place for up to 2 months.

Tips *If you should make your own homemade kefir, sprinkle a couple of drops into the brine in the preserving jar, as it will help the good bacteria grow. Watch out for infections, as beetroot is quite prone to it. But it's not a problem if the celery becomes a little mouldy by the end of the process – just chuck it away.*

Pickled cherries and the gang

We mostly ferment in Ukraine and Georgia, so I'm a little funny about vinegar pickles, as I often find them too strong, but in Azerbaijan they do use vinegar for pickling and do fantastic things with the pickles. Pickled cherries were a huge revelation to me – they are simply to die for. They are also extremely easy to make and this way of pickling can be used for many fruits and vegetables. Try this with cauliflower florets, grapes, cucumbers or, less traditionally, daikon, thinly sliced crab apples or fennel. These are great served with some buttery *plov* (see pages 120 and 128) and a rich lamb or duck dish, or Lyulya Kebabs (see page 152).

Makes a 1-litre (1¾-pint) jar
  300ml (10fl/½ pint) cider vinegar
  100ml (3½fl oz) water
  20g (¾oz) granulated sugar
  10g (¼oz) fine sea salt
  5 garlic cloves, peeled and halved
  500g (1lb 2oz) yellow, red, cornel or sour cherries, or grapes

  You will also need a sterilized 1-litre (1¾-pint) preserving jar

Put the vinegar, water, sugar and salt into a non-reactive pan and bring to the boil slowly, stirring all the time, so that the sugar dissolves before the water boils.

Turn off the heat, leave to cool and add the garlic.

Pour the pickling liquid over your cherries, or other fruit or vegetables, packed into your sterilized preserving jar, seal and leave to pickle in the refrigerator for at least a couple of hours. They can be kept in the pickling liquid in the refrigerator for up to a month.

Caucasus is not the place to find a great variety of puddings. Of course, Soviet-era cakes are still made and adapted all over, but as a rule, especially in Azerbaijan, fruit, nuts and sweet preserves served with a hot strong tea are the norm. There are many types of *pakhlava*, including the most beautiful lace *pakhlava* from Shekhi (west of Azerbaijan) made with rice flour; there are *khalvas* and Georgian and Armenian *churchkhela* (nuts covered in grape must), but there isn't much else. And I don't mind that. Often, after a big feast, I do not feel like a heavy cake. But do not skip this chapter – I have collected plenty of recipes for those who are sweet in the tooth.

sweet in the tooth

Pakhlava

Pakhlava is a festive dish made for *Novruz*, the traditional celebration of the coming of spring in Azerbaijan, but it's rarely prepared at home, since nuts are expensive and making thin pastry is rather laborious. However, it is a gorgeous thing, and if you like baking and making something new, this is a great way to spend an afternoon, especially if you are cooking with your loved ones. The recipe makes enough to last you a couple of weeks and to package up into gift boxes for friends and family.

Makes about 55 pieces

400–500g (14oz–1lb 2oz) Clarified Butter (see page 53), for brushing

2 eggs, beaten, for glazing

nut pieces, for decorating

DOUGH

2 eggs

200g (7oz) unsalted butter, melted

200g (7oz) soured cream

10g (¼oz) caster sugar

3g (½ teaspoon) fast-action dried yeast

pinch of salt

800g (1lb 12oz) plain flour, plus extra for dusting

SYRUP

175ml (6fl oz) water

50g (1lb 2oz) caster sugar

a pinch of saffron threads

FILLING

800g (1lb 12oz) nuts (walnuts, almonds and pistachios are all equally good), ground, plus about 55 pieces of nut to decorate

600g (1lb 5oz) caster sugar

15g (½oz) cardamom pods, toasted and seeds ground

You will also need a baking tray measuring 25 x 40cm (10 x 16 inches)

To make the dough, mix the eggs with the melted butter, soured cream, sugar and yeast in a large bowl. Mix the salt into the flour, then gradually add the flour to the bowl, first mixing with a wooden spoon and then working the mixture with your hands into a firm dough. Cover with a damp tea towel and leave to rest for 30 minutes.

For the syrup, put the water, sugar and saffron into a pan and bring to the boil slowly, stirring all the time, so that the sugar dissolves before the water starts boiling. Leave to cool.

Mix all the filling ingredients together in a bowl and set aside.

Divide the dough into 8 balls – 2 of them (for the top and bottom layer) should be 350g (12oz) each, the other 6 should be 100g (3½oz) each.

Line the baking tray with baking parchment, with enough excess all round so that you can use it to manipulate and lift the *pakhlava* out, and brush the paper with Clarified Butter.

Flour your work surface and press one of the 350g (12oz) pieces of dough down with your hand into a disc. Then using a (preferably) thin rolling pin, roll the dough into a 25 x 40cm (10 x 16-inch) rectangle and place it on the lined tray. Brush with Clarified Butter and sprinkle over some of the filling.

Roll out each 100g (3½oz) piece of dough, one by one, as thinly as you can into the same size rectangle as before and then layer into the tray, again brushing each sheet of dough with the Clarified Butter and adding a sprinkling of the filling.

Roll out the remaining 350g (12oz) piece of dough to fit the tray and pop it on top of the other layers. Press the *pakhlava* gently with the palm of your hand. Now grab the ends of the baking parchment and swiftly fold them over the dough and bring them back again in order to tidy up the shape of the *pakhlava*. Do the same with each side and then twist each corner of the parchment to make it easier to lift the whole thing out once baked.

Cut it lengthways into 7 vertical strips, and then into 12 on the diagonal to create about 55 diamonds – enough to last you a couple of weeks and make gift boxes for friends and family

Preheat the oven to 200°C (400°F), Gas Mark 6. Brush the top of the *pakhlava* with the egg glaze and press a piece of nut into the middle of each diamond. Bake for 15–20 minutes, then remove from the oven and drizzle over the rest of the Clarified Butter. Lower the temperature of the oven to 180°C (350°F), Gas Mark 4 and return to the oven for another 25 minutes until the top layer is golden and crispy.

Take the *pakhlava* out of the oven and drizzle over the saffron syrup, then go over the cuts again with a knife and drizzle the syrup between the layers, too. Leave the *pakhlava* to settle for a bit, then lift it out carefully (like a body on a stretcher) using the twisted baking parchment corners with somebody's help. Run along the cuts again and then store the pieces in an airtight container, out of the refrigerator for up to a week, or in the refrigerator for up to a month; if the latter, make sure you take it out 2 hours before serving so that the Clarified Butter isn't too hard.

Nana's pine cone muffins

Marina Nariashvili runs her own guest house in Akhaltsikhe in southern Georgia, as well as creating all sorts of incredible things from pine cones. Her daughter-in-law Nana also makes really excellent food and possesses one of the most serene, beautiful faces I have ever encountered; gentle but strong, as if out of a painting. This is one of Nana's recipes, although I must admit that the original had twice as much sugar. I prefer them less sweet, especially if they are dipped in the cocoa dulce de leche sauce. But if you aren't serving them with the sauce, please do add more sugar.

Makes 12 muffins

150g (5½oz) caster sugar

1 eggs

175g (6oz) Homemade Matsoni (see page 29) or natural yogurt

2 tablespoons sunflower oil

200g (7oz) plain flour

1 teaspoons bicarbonate of soda

½ teaspoon baking powder

12 small young green pine cones (optional)

Clementine Preserve juice (see page 210), to glaze

DIPPING SAUCE

200g (7oz) unsalted butter

250g (9oz) dulce de leche or Anna's Sweet Milk (see page 220)

3 tablespoons caster sugar

5 tablespoons cocoa powder

Preheat the oven to 180°C (350°F), Gas Mark 4. Lightly oil a 12-cup muffin tray or line with paper cases.

Beat the sugar and eggs together in a bowl until light and fluffy, then fold in the Homemade Matsoni or yogurt and the oil.

In a separate bowl, sift the flour with the bicarbonate of soda and baking powder, then fold into the liquid ingredients.

Fill the paper cases a little more than ⅔ full with the muffin mixture, then bake in the oven for about 30 minutes until well risen and golden brown. Five minutes before the end of the baking time, add a pine cone to the top of each muffin, if using, and brush with some Clementine Preserve juice to glaze. Remove the muffins from the oven and leave to cool slightly on a wire rack.

For the dipping sauce, mix all the ingredients together in a saucepan, set over a low heat and stir just until the mixture has completely melted – don't cook it for any longer. Dip the tops of the muffins into the sauce and serve straight away.

Pine flower honey

It's springtime again and Marina heads out to collect pine flower buds. They are covered in a little "skirt", which is removed and then the flower buds pounded, their golden dust (pollen) showering everywhere. Marina gives pine cone flower honey to her grandchildren every morning, as it's believed to be beneficial for the lungs. Try this honey on pancakes!

Makes a 1kg (2lb 4-oz) jar
  500g (1lb 2oz) pine flower buds
  750g (1lb 10oz) wild flower honey

  You will also need a 1kg (2lb 4oz) clean airtight jar

Mince the flowers in a meat mincer, if you have one, or bash them using a pestle and mortar.

Mix the minced or pounded flowers through the honey until well incorporated.

Pour the honey into the jar, seal and store in a cool, dry place.

Pine cone conserve

Marina Nariashvili's guest house in southern Georgia is surrounded by pine forests. Her many grandchildren all have little blankets for taking a nap under the pine trees during the day or to meditate, in the lotus position in the case of her eight-year-old granddaughter! Come May, Marina ventures deeper into the forest to forage for little young pine cones to turn into all sorts of wonderful things, including this conserve. Serve it with drop scones or with the Pine Cone Muffins (see page 195).

Makes 3.5kg (7lb 10oz)
  1 litre (1¾ pints) water
  1.5kg (3lb 5oz) granulated sugar
  1kg (2lb 4oz) young green pine cones
  1 teaspoon citric acid

  You will also need a sugar thermometer

Put the water into a large pan, add the sugar and heat gently, stirring, until dissolved.

Add the pine cones and continue cooking the syrup until it reaches a temperature of 112–116°C (234–240°F) on the thermometer, or soft-ball stage, which will take about 30 minutes.

Add the citric acid, then leave the mixture to cool before using. If the syrup is too liquid once cooled, reheat and cook for a few minutes more. It will store unopened for a few months.

Armenian "cognac" profiteroles

There was something about Soviet-era Armenian "cognac". It was actually just a brandy and I'm not sure how good it really was, probably not very. I normally hate desserts with alcohol, which must be down to the bad-quality chocolates filled with sickly sour cherry liqueur that we were all too familiar with growing up, but there was and still is one exception – my mum's profiteroles that she would lace with lashings of this cognac when we were little. My mum doesn't even remember that she used to make them and in fact now denies she ever did! But I will never forget that lovely hit of alcohol in luscious crème mousseline made with raw milk and thickened with butter. The choux pastry recipe is based on the one that I was taught at Leiths School of Food and Wine and it is foolproof. If you can't find Armenian brandy, use a little dash of Armagnac. Or try a splash of Tia Maria – almost as classy as the Armenian stuff! Sarcasm aside, it does deliver an amazing, subtle flavour and is also very good used in a tiramisu.

Makes approx. 12 large profiteroles

CHOUX PASTRY

220ml (7¾fl oz) water

85g (3oz) unsalted butter, cut into cubes

105g (3¾oz) plain flour

pinch of salt

3 eggs, at room temperature, lightly beaten

CRÈME MOUSSELINE

450ml (16fl oz) milk

1 vanilla pod, split lengthways and seeds scraped out, pod reserved

5 egg yolks

100g (3½oz) caster sugar

75g (2¾oz) plain flour

50ml (2fl oz) Armenian brandy or equivalent (your favourite)

50g (1¾oz) unsalted butter, cut into pieces

Preheat the oven to 200°C (400°F), Gas Mark 6. Line 2 large baking sheets with baking parchment.

To make the choux pastry, put the water and butter into a saucepan and warm it over a low heat so that the butter melts but the water doesn't boil and evaporate.

Sift the flour over a sheet of baking parchment, then fold and seal one end of the paper to create a pocket. You basically have to dump all the flour in one go into the hot water (we called it "bombing it"), and this makes it easier. So with your flour pocket and a wooden spoon at the ready, raise the heat under the pan and wait for the water to boil and rise, and the butter to be collected in the centre. Shoot the flour in, switch off the heat and beat the mixture with a wooden spoon until it starts separating from the walls of the pan, turning into a ball.

continued »

Spread the mixture over a large plate to help it cool down. Then pop it into a bowl and start beating in the eggs, 1 tablespoon at a time. You are looking for a shiny dough with a reluctant dropping consistency. When one-third of the egg has gone in, lift a bit of dough up on the edge of the wooden spoon and let it drop – it should take 6 seconds for it to drop if the consistency is right.

Spoon large tablespoonfuls of the choux mixture on to the lined baking sheets, allowing some space in between, as the pastry will expand during baking.

Bake for 25–30 minutes or until the choux buns are golden and cooked through. Remove from the oven and leave them to cool on a wire rack.

Meanwhile, to make the alcoholic crème mousseline, heat the milk with the vanilla seeds and scraped-out pod in a large saucepan.

Mix the egg yolks with the sugar and the flour in a separate bowl.

When the milk is near boiling point, quickly tip some of it into the egg mixture, stirring vigorously so that the eggs don't scramble. Then tip the egg mixture into the rest of the milk in the pan and cook over a medium-low heat, stirring constantly, for about 10–15 minutes or until the cream thickens to a custard-like consistency.

Add the alcohol and turn off the heat, then add the butter, a piece at a time, whisking to help it melt. Cover the surface with clingfilm to stop a skin from forming, then leave it to cool completely.

When everything is cooled and you are ready to serve, make a hole at the bottom of each choux bun and fill with the crème mousseline.

VARIATION
You can drizzle melted chocolate ganache over the profiteroles, or try dipping them in the cocoa and dulce de leche dipping sauce as with the Pine Cone Muffins (see page 195).

I have tried filling these with the custard for the Buckwheat Ice Cream (see pages 202–3) with some flour and butter added as per the recipe above and it was interesting and delicious. And instead of chocolate, I brushed the profiteroles with a little sugar syrup and sprinkled over some toasted buckwheat groats.

Preserved whole peaches

In the Ukraine, we would preserve our summer glut in exactly the same way, producing the best "canned" (or rather bottled) fruit known to humanity. Forget the stuff you buy in cans – this is the real deal. Look for the best end-of-summer produce available and then enjoy the resulting preserved fruits and their fragrant syrup just as they come, biting into the flesh with the juice dribbling down your chin, or in cakes. Dan Lepard devised an amazing cake recipe using canned peaches and almonds that I have been using for years. So here is how you can make this sensuous, *callypigian* preserve.

Makes a 3-litre (5¼-pint) jar
   2 litres (3½ pints) water
   500g (1lb 2oz) golden caster sugar
   7 ripe but firm peaches, left whole

   You will also need a sterilized 3-litre (5¼-pint) preserving jar

Put the water into a large pan, add the sugar and heat gently, stirring, until dissolved, then bring to the boil.

Pop the peaches into your sterilized jar – the fruits will hopefully be small enough to be pushed through the neck of the jar. Pour over the hot syrup and leave to cool. When cool, pour the syrup out of the jar into a saucepan (leaving the peaches in the jar) and reheat the syrup again to boiling point, then pour it back over the peaches one more time.

Seal hermetically if you can.

Buckwheat ice cream

I really really wanted to use Marina's pine cones in a dessert of my own (see pages 195–6), as they are just so unusual, a chef's dream. But because they are so tannic and taste so strongly of pine, only a tiny bit could be used. I also really wanted to make buckwheat ice cream, as when we were children, mum used to boil buckwheat in salted water and then dress it with melted butter and sugar. That flavour was haunting me, just like I imagine the cereal milk would for those who grew up eating sweet cereal. My friend Alissa and I threw a Kino Vino supper club during Russian filmmaker Andrei Tarkovsky Week in London, showing his 1975 film called *Mirror*, followed by a feast inspired by the movie. One of the last scenes depicted a buckwheat field bordering a malachite-hued pine forest. Bingo. The two came together. So this is my poetic nostalgic dessert, although don't worry about trying to find pine cones, as I've suggested using fresh bay leaves instead here to add savouriness.

Serves 6–8

100g (3½oz) raw buckwheat groats
(or use ready-toasted)

10 fresh bay leaves, crushed

250ml (9fl oz) milk

250g (9oz) double cream

generous pinch of salt

150g (5½oz) caster sugar (optional)

4 egg yolks

100–150g (3½–5½oz) granulated sugar

poached rhubarb, to serve

You will also need (ideally) an ice-cream
machine and a large piece of muslin

If using raw buckwheat, heat a large, dry frying pan over a medium heat, toss in the buckwheat and toast, wiggling the pan about from time to time, until it becomes golden but not burnt. Taste it and check that it is crunchy and edible – it's very important that you get this right. Leave the buckwheat to cool.

Wrap the crushed bay leaves and buckwheat in the muslin and tie securely. Add it to the milk and cream in a large saucepan over a medium heat. Add the salt and taste the mixture – you should be able to detect the salt ever so slightly. If you intend to serve the ice cream with something tart, add 150g (5½oz) caster sugar.

When the milk mixture is almost boiling, turn the heat off and leave to infuse for an hour.

Beat the egg yolks and sugar together in a large heatproof bowl.

Remove the muslin and squeeze out all the flavour, then discard. Bring the milk mixture back up to almost boiling. Pour it on to the egg yolk mixture, stirring constantly, then pour this mixture back into the pan and cook over a low heat, stirring, for about 5 minutes or until slightly thickened.

Cover the surface of the custard with clingfilm to prevent a skin from forming and leave the custard to cool.

Churn the ice cream in an ice-cream machine according to the manufacturer's instructions, then serve with some simple poached rhubarb.

Tip If you don't have an ice-cream machine, create a semifreddo with the custard. Make the custard as instructed above and leave to cool, then fold through 4 egg whites, whisked until firm peaks form. Freeze for 2 hours and serve slightly soft.

Qata

Versions of this biscuit recipe exist all over the Caucasus. I was taught this one by my Aunt Nina on the Armenian side of the family. She makes them plain, but I do love nuts in my biscuits, so I add either whole or crushed nuts to the buttery filling. My mum also sprinkles sesame seeds over them because, well, any biscuit or bread is improved by the addition of sesame in our opinion.

Makes 30–35 biscuits

PASTRY

400g (14oz) plain flour, plus extra for dusting

10g (¼oz) baking powder

pinch of salt

1 egg, lightly beaten

150g (5½oz) soured cream

1 teaspoon vanilla extract

250g (9oz) butter, frozen and coarsely grated

FILLING

200g (7oz) unsalted butter, frozen and coarsely grated

200g (7oz) caster sugar

1 vanilla pod, split lengthways and seeds scraped out

150g (5½oz) plain flour

50g (1¾oz) pecan nuts, toasted and crushed

GLAZE

1 egg yolk, lightly beaten

20g (¾oz) sesame seeds

To make the pastry, mix the flour, baking powder and salt together in a bowl.

Mix the egg, soured cream and vanilla extract together.

Add the butter to the flour mixture and rub in with your fingertips until the mixture looks like crumbs. Mix in the egg and soured cream mixture and quickly knead into a dough, then cover with clingfilm and refrigerate for an hour or so.

To make the filling, mix the grated butter, sugar and vanilla seeds together. Put the flour in a bowl, add the butter mixture and rub in as you did for the pastry.

Preheat the oven to 180°C (350°F), Gas Mark 4. Dust 2 baking sheets with flour.

Divide the pastry in half. Working quickly, flatten each half with your hand and then roll out on a floured work surface into a sheet 5mm (¼ inch) thick.

Mix the pecan nuts into the filling and spread it over each pastry sheet (or dot it around evenly if your dough is too soft and delicate), leaving a narrow border around the edges.

Roll each pastry sheet up into a long sausage as firmly as you can, manipulating the sausage so it is the same thickness all the way along. Put it into the refrigerator for 15 minutes to firm up.

Position the sausages seam side down on your work surface, then brush with the beaten egg yolk and sprinkle over the sesame seeds. Dip a knife in hot water and slice each sausage into 2cm (¾-inch) thick discs. Place the discs flat on the prepared baking sheets 8cm (3¼ inches) apart and squash them slightly with your hands. Put back into the refrigerator for 30 minutes – if they are firm before baking they will hold their shape better. Bake for 25–30 minutes until golden brown. Leave to cool a little on a wire rack and serve warm.

Three-ears with khalva khasan

It has been really quite difficult to find dessert recipes for this book. Caucasus people simply don't have a prominent baking culture. Sweet strong tea or fruit (fresh or dried), jams and nuts are what you have at the end of a meal. So whenever I met anyone on my travels in the region, I would really try to tickle their memory to see if they recalled anything special from their childhood. When I visited a family in the hills of Qebele with their endless chestnut trees, it turned out that they made sweet samosas with filo pastry filled with walnut and sugar paste. But then Halima, the 80-year-old babushka, remembered what she called *khalva khasan* as her favourite, rare childhood treat. She described it as a paste made using chestnuts, hazelnuts and sugar. The three-eared samosa provides the perfect shell for this *khalva khasan*.

Makes 24
- 120g (4¼oz) cooked and peeled chestnuts or vacuum-packed
- 60g (2¼oz) hazelnuts, toasted
- 60g (2¼oz) walnuts, toasted
- 60g (2¼oz) granulated sugar
- 1 vanilla pod, split lengthways and seeds scraped out
- 240g (8½oz) filo pastry sheets (about 6 sheets)
- 100g (3½oz) unsalted butter, melted
- 2 egg yolks mixed with 1 tablespoon milk, to glaze

Preheat the oven to 180°C (350°F), Gas Mark 4.

First, pound all the nuts, sugar and vanilla seeds together using a pestle and mortar, or blitz in a powerful blender or food processor, to a paste. Your filling is ready.

Keeping the filo sheets covered by a damp tea towel so that they don't dry out, take one sheet and lay it on the work surface in front of you with the shorter edge nearest you. Brush it lightly with melted butter, then slice it vertically into 4 long strips.

Place a tablespoonful of the filling at the bottom of each strip and fold the bottom right-hand corner up, over the filling. Then do the same with the bottom left-hand corner. Continue folding the strip in triangles until you reach the top and you have a beautiful little samosa. Repeat with the rest of the filo and filling to make 24 dainty pastries.

Place the pastries on a large baking sheet, brush with the egg yolk mixture to glaze and bake for 8 minutes or until golden and crisp. Serve with some strong black tea. Store any left over in an airtight container – they should keep up for up to 1 week.

Valya's lemon tart

Azerbaijani cuisine is not renowned for its desserts, so Zulfiya was fortunate in having Valentina, a Russian woman, as a family friend who makes sweet creations. She may have had an influence on Zulya, who besides being a concert pianist and piano teacher at a conservatory in Baku is now also a pastry shop owner, as she gives her desserts musical names, thereby bringing both her worlds together. I am giving the original recipe here, which features the use of vinegar, an acid, as a catalyst for the bicarbonate of soda to act as a raising agent. This technique was widely used in the Soviet Union because yeast was often scarce.

This is a strong-tasting dessert, so have a small piece with a cup of strong tea without milk.

Serves 6–8
3–4 large lemons
250g (9oz) caster sugar
2 egg yolks, beaten, to glaze

PASTRY
225g (8oz) plain flour
generous pinch of salt
100g (3½oz) cold unsalted butter, diced
1 teaspoon cider vinegar
½ teaspoon bicarbonate of soda

For the pastry, sift the flour and salt together into a large bowl, then rub in the cold butter until the mixture resembles fine breadcrumbs. Alternatively, chill the flour in a container in the refrigerator and then add the salt and blitz it with the cold butter in a food processor.

Add the vinegar to the bicarbonate of soda, which will make it foam, then add a splash of water. Mix the liquid into the flour and butter mixture to bind it into a dough. Wrap the dough in clingfilm and chill in the refrigerator for at least an hour.

Cover the lemons with boiling water and leave for 20 minutes, then drain and leave to cool. Place them in the freezer for at least 2 hours until frozen.

Preheat the oven to 180°C (350°F), Gas Mark 4.

Use the pastry to line a 24cm (9½ inch) tart tin. Line the pastry case with baking parchment, fill with ceramic baking beans and bake blind for 5 minutes, then remove the beans and paper and bake for another 5 minutes.

Remove the lemons from the freezer and grate them coarsely (this will be hard and cold, but hang in there!). Mix the grated lemons with the sugar, then use to fill the pastry case. Use a pastry brush to dab with the egg glaze. Bake for 35–40 minutes until the filling has set to a marmalade-like consistency. Leave to cool before serving.

Clementine preserve

Clementines and mandarins were in huge deficit when I was growing up, a special treat reserved for Christmas. I clearly remember burying myself in yet another book under a scratchy blanket sucking the juice out of every segment of a clementine, then chewing on the empty membrane, one by one until all the mandarins I nicked from the kitchen were gone and I had to procure another tasty snack. Reading and eating were the biggest pleasures in my life at that point. Those precious clementines were from the southwestern Georgian region of Adjara, a mountainous tropical beauty of a land, with rows and rows of clementine and Sharon fruit trees. They make a pretty simple clementine preserve there, still juicy and not too sweet, and here's my version – a new favourite way to eat this fruit.

Makes 650g (1lb 7oz)

   500g (1lb 2oz) clementines

   300g (10½oz) caster sugar

   300ml (10½fl oz) water

   1 cinnamon stick

   juice of ½ lemon

   You will also need 3 x 225g (8oz) sterilized airtight jars

Cover the whole, unpeeled clementines with cold water in a bowl and leave to soak overnight.

The next morning, cut the clementines in half along the equator and then into half moons 5mm (¼ inch) thick.

Add the sugar and water to the fruit and again leave overnight.

Transfer the entire contents of the bowl to a medium saucepan along with the cinnamon and cook over a low heat for 1¼ hours.

Add the lemon juice and cook for another 15 minutes or until set to your liking.

Pour the hot preserve into the warm sterilized jars, seal and leave to cool, then store in cool, dark place. It should keep unopened for up to a year.

Tip Marina from Akhaltsikhe rolls the citrus peel into pretty little curls before jarring – an example of intense marmalade dedication that I've never seen before.

Tarragon & cucumber lemonade

Instead of cola and fizzy orange drinks, us ex-Soviet children grew up drinking a fizzy fluorescent green pop called *tarkhun*, meaning "tarragon". It was poisonous-green, very sweet yet somehow delicious. Tarragon is extremely popular in Georgia – they do not shy away from its strong flavour. I do love the addition of cucumbers like they do in the Pheasant's Tears restaurant in Signagi, a town in the Kakheti region of eastern Georgia, which makes this summer drink even fresher.

Makes about 3 litres (5¼ pints)
    500ml (18fl oz) water
    200g (7oz) caster sugar
    finely grated zest and juice of 4 (preferably Sicilian) lemons
    2 bunches of tarragon
    2 cucumbers, sliced
    2 litres (3½ pints) cold sparkling mineral water

Put the still water into a saucepan with the sugar and heat over a low heat, stirring often, until the sugar has completely dissolved. Leave to cool completely, then stir in the lemon zest and juice.

Blitz the tarragon (reserving a few sprigs) and half the cucumber in a blender or food processor (easier and less splashy than using a pestle and mortar, although you can do it that way). Strain the mixture through a fine sieve.

Mix the lemony cordial with the tarragon and cucumber juice and dilute it as you would with any cordial – topped up with sparkling or still water. This is not too bad with a dash of gin, too.

Tklapi or plum fruit leather

Fruit leathers are a big thing in the Caucasus. It is simply another way to preserve a glut of fruit and every kind is used, from small tart plums to mulberries, cherries, apricots and even kiwifruit. They make a beautiful healthy snack, but also add a subtle sweet and sour note to stews and soups. In Akhaltsikhe, a small city in southern Georgia, I visited Galina's house and found her holding a giant oar of a wooden spoon that she was using to stir about 20 litres (4½ gallons) of plum pulp in a huge cauldron on top of a wood fire. It was mid-afternoon and still hot even though it was the end of September. Galina was reducing the liquid until it thickened and was almost syrupy. Her daughters-in-law and little grandson were there to help and cover the long outside table with white linen sheets. They poured the hot purée on top of the linen sheets and spread it into a thin layer. It was left to set and dry in the sun, hanging over a washing line. When dry, it is unpeeled and folded, and kept over winter in a dark, dry place.

Makes two 30 x 40cm (12 x 16-inch) sheets
  1kg (2lb 4oz) ripe plums (or apricots, apples, mulberries, strawberries or cherries)
  50g (1¾oz) caster sugar or honey (adjust depending on how sweet the fruit is)
  juice of 1 lemon

Put your plums into a large stockpot or preserving pan and add a splash of water. Heat over a medium heat until the mixture starts bubbling, then reduce the heat and cook for about 30 minutes or until the plums have collapsed. Stir from time to time, and if it looks like there isn't enough moisture, add another splash of water. Strain through a fine-mesh sieve into a large bowl, discarding the stones and skin.

Place the plum flesh back in the cleaned pan, add the sugar or honey and lemon juice and cook over a low heat until the sugar, if using, has dissolved, then simmer for about 40 minutes– 1 hour. You are aiming for a smooth and thick purée about 600g (1lb 5 oz) in quantity.

Meanwhile, preheat the oven to 100°C (212°F/lowest Gas mark) and line 2 large baking trays with nonstick baking parchment.

Ladle some of the hot fruit purée all over the lined trays, then spread it thinly – the fruit leather should be almost transparent. Leave it to dry in the oven for about 12 hours. The leather should be thoroughly dry and peel away from the parchment easily. Then just fold it into quarters and wrap in baking parchment. It will keep somewhere dark and dry for 6 months.

Tip This method can be applied to most types of fruit, as the whole point of the recipe is to preserve overripe, surplus fruit in September – it just has to be of good quality and very ripe.

Basil sherbet

They love a sherbet in Azerbaijan. It is basically an infused fruit or spiced sugar syrup diluted with cold water.

Makes 1 litre (1¾ pints)
- 1 litre (1¾ pints) hot water
- 1 bunch of purple or green basil, or Thai basil, leaves and stalks separated
- juice of 4 lemons, plus extra to taste
- 100g (3½oz) agave syrup, plus extra to taste
- crushed ice, to serve

Pour the hot (but not boiling) water over the basil stalks in a bowl and leave to stand and infuse until it cools down. The water will turn purple if using purple basil!

Mix the lemon juice with the agave syrup in a separate bowl, then add the basil leaves and muddle them together a little.

Strain the stalks out of the water and then stir the infused water into the lemon and basil leaf mixture. Taste it and add more lemon or agave as you wish. Serve with some crushed ice.

Keti's tea

Irish coffee? Try Georgian tea. In the Kazbegi mountains in northeastern Georgia, Keti gave us some herbal tea. I couldn't put my finger on why this herbal tea was so incredible. I kept drinking it, with my eyes getting wider and wider. "What is this? Is this some kind of crazy wild berry?" I asked Keti. She smiled wryly – it turns out that she had sweetened it with vanilla sugar and spiked it with brandy!

Don't worry if you can't find exactly the same dried wild herbs – any combination of aromatics will work. It is the addition of brandy and vanilla that turns this tea into something quite delicious.

Serves 4–6
- 5g (⅛oz) dried wild thyme
- 10g (¼oz) rosehips
- 5g (⅛oz) dried barberries
- 5g (⅛oz) black tea leaves
- handful of dried citrus peel
- ¼ vanilla pod or 1 tablespoon vanilla sugar
- splash of good brandy

Pop everything except the brandy into a teapot and cover with boiling water.

Leave to infuse for about 5 minutes, then add the brandy.

Anna's sweet milk

A lady I met called Zhuzhuna Bardzimadze from Akhaltsikhe had the kindest face and tastiest pickles. She lives, like so many others in Georgia, with her son and Kakhetian daughter-in-law Anna. Anna makes the sweetest milk – a proper homemade dulce de leche, and by that I don't mean boiling shop-bought condensed milk! This is the real deal. I loved that she knew that the amount the recipe made would vary depending on the season, due to the difference in the fat content of the milk. In August, for instance, her yield was always bigger, as the milk is fattier. The Georgians make cakes with this or just eat it spread on a bit of bread.

Makes approx. 700ml (1¼ pints)
  2 litres (3½ pints) cows' milk or goats' milk
  350g (12oz) caster sugar
  1 vanilla pod, split lengthways and seeds scraped out
  1 teaspoon sea salt flakes
  1 teaspoon bicarbonate of soda

Bring the milk and sugar to the boil in a large saucepan (it needs to be a tall saucepan, as the milk will rise and froth once the soda is added).

Take the pan off the heat and add the bicarbonate of soda. Stir it and it will start to foam and rise rapidly (tap the base of the pan with a wooden spoon to stop it).

When it calms down, put the pan back on the heat and continue to boil over a low heat, stirring from time to time to ensure it doesn't catch on the bottom, and taking care not to let it boil or the milk can curdle. Cook for for 30–40 minutes until the milk turns darker in colour (it should look like café au lait colour at this point). When the mixture thickens and is the consistency of double cream, really watch it and start whisking continuously to prevent curdling. As it thickens, keep whisking until it reduces right down. Once the mixture has become viscous and brown like toasted hazelnuts, it's ready.

Tip If the mixture looks curdled, it can be saved by reheating and whisking in a couple of tablespoons of milk.

Opposite: Zhuzhuna and her son.

Liliana's lemon & dulce de leche cake

Elena, the book's photographer, is half-Argentinian. When Anna brought along a jar of her homemade condensed milk, Elena's face lit up. "I know my dulce de leche," she remarked with a twinkle in her eye and a wry smile. She tried it and smiled again, declaring, "It's good, it's very good!" And then she told me that her mum Liliana made a lemon and dulce de leche cake, which sounded so good. It turned out even better, as there was a suitably sweet story attached to it. It's about Liliana's third child Hanry, who was born between lunch and this cake on 1 October 1989. It goes like this, in her own words: "Contractions started in the morning, so I thought I should bake a cake, as Dr Michel Odent was coming to assist me. I went shopping so that I had all the ingredients, I made the cake and my mother prepared lunch. Sunday lunch... I was so hungry! But when the lemon and dulce de leche cake was approaching the table, I stood up and shouted: 'No cake, baby is coming!' And I took refuge in a bedroom. Only an hour and a half later, my 9lb (4kg) boy was born. At this point I asked his father: 'Could you hold the baby so that I can eat the cake?' And he replied: 'I would love to... but the cord is short...!' I was still attached to the baby, as the placenta had not yet been delivered!" This story made me happy. The end.

Serves 6–8

- grated zest and juice of 1 lemon
- 10g (¼oz) lemon verbena leaves, bruised (optional)
- 20g (¾oz) icing sugar
- 200g (7oz) unsalted butter, softened, plus extra for greasing
- 200g (7oz) caster sugar
- 2 eggs, lightly beaten
- 200g (7oz) self-raising flour
- 200ml (7fl oz) dulce de leche or Anna's Sweet Milk (see page 220)
- edible flowers, such as borage or cornflowers, to decorate

To make the drizzle, mix the lemon juice with the bruised verbena leaves, if using, in a bowl and leave to infuse for at least 30 minutes. Then whisk in the icing sugar, making sure that it dissolves.

Preheat the oven to 180°C (350°C), Gas Mark 4. Grease a 22cm (8½-inch) cake tin and line it with baking parchment.

Using an electric whisk or a stand mixer fitted with a paddle attachment, beat the butter and caster sugar together until really pale and fluffy. Then gradually add the eggs and the lemon zest, beating well after each addition.

Fold the flour through the cake mixture gently, then pour the cake mixture into the prepared tin. Bake for 30 minutes or until a skewer comes out clean.

Leave the cake to cool in the tin for a few minutes, then turn out on to a wire rack, remove the lining paper and leave to cool completely.

Cut the cake in half horizontally and spread the dulce de leche on the bottom layer, then cover with the top layer. Brush the drizzle over the top of the cake (it will soak in), scatter with edible flowers to decorate and serve.

kaukasis

II   Dedakatsi – the "mother-man"

Dedakatsi – the "mother-man"

My whole life I have been fascinated and even slightly obsessed with strong women. I wouldn't be able to describe what life was like pre-1939, extremely tough I imagine, but it seems to me that World War II, coupled with the atrocities committed by the Soviet Union, has produced a generation of women that could move mountains.

When somebody told me the meaning of the word *dedakatsi* in Georgia, which literally translates as "mother-man", it was almost an epiphany.

My grandfather Viktor, who escaped concentration camps and was imprisoned for a couple of years by the Soviets, was a quiet man. Gentle by nature, he was forced to retreat further into a withdrawn and subdued state following what happened to him in the 1930s and '40s. I remember seeing him quietly sitting on his chair in the kitchen when we visited, while my grandmother Lusia, a formidable force with the straightest back I've ever seen, was running around cooking, taking care of the farm animals and looking after their six children. Vitechka with his James Dean golden locks and piercing blue eyes would just be having a toke on his filterless Prima cigarette, sipping on a glass of homemade wine if my grandmother felt benevolent enough that day to let him. He never talked about what happened to him during the war; the trauma of it must have been too great. And Lusia was a true matriarch; not in the sense recognized by society as such, but she really was.

And this was a familiar pattern that I have come across throughout Georgia. Of course, there have been tons of incredibly talented, strong and hard-working men that I've met. But it struck me how many women were so much like Lusia, if more self-sacrificial, and not all of them were my grandmother's generation or even near. This is not feminism in the way that we all strive to achieve in the West, but altogether a different notion. This is women doing everything, so not exactly the equality that feminism represents. But it's no less admirable.

Visiting the incredible Georgian vineyards, I've experienced the remarkable achievements of the relatively recent pioneers of organic winemaking, the men that take pride and glory in producing their natural, ancient qvevri wines. They are saving one of the oldest traditions known to man, so to me they might as well be saving the world. But what people don't talk about as much are the women behind these men. I have witnessed wives and 87-year-old mothers staying up until 1am, cooking and serving, so that their husbands and sons could entertain potential wine ex-porters or food and drink writers. And those women also often work the vineyards, have other jobs besides and raise children. They are superwomen. In no way am I passing judgement, but all the work they do at the vineyards and beyond should be recognized and highly respected. And the *dedakatsi* role is not exclusive to the winemaking world – I have seen it fulfilled in many houses and not just in Georgia.

The journey

On 3 July 1986, on a whim, my parents packed my ten-year-old brother and me
into an old Zhiguli and we set off on a journey to Azerbaijan's capital city
of Baku. My father's uncle, Stepan Grebenyuk, was married to Tamara Balasanova,
an Armenian with roots in Karabakh, the now disputed area in southwestern
Azerbaijan, and my dad had lived with them in Baku during the year of his parents'
tragic divorce when he was a teenager. He loved both them and the city dearly.

It took us two hours to reach Crimea from our home town of Kakhovka in
southern Ukraine, and only then did we realize that we hadn't actually told our
Bakunian family that we were coming, so a telegram(!) was swiftly dispatched.
We then loaded our stuffy Zhiguli "brick" on to a ferry and slowly chugged
along the Black Sea towards the exoticism of Sochi. My mum still talks about
the palm trees, the alleys, the beaches… it was like entering another universe.
We kept moving, the sweltering dry air and winding roads making me feel ill, my
parents cursing their wanderlust. Finally we stopped in Abkhazia by some picturesque
lakes. A modest old tent was erected and a couple of foldable chairs and a tiny
table set up, then we fried some sausages over a camp fire before it was time to rest.

On we drove through the Georgian hills, through the western region of Samegrelo
down to sub-tropical Batumi. We got lost in Tbilisi, the Georgian capital, and
had to ask a man in a car to direct us towards the motorway. My mother still
remembers his kindness – even though he was going the opposite direction to us,
he took us all the way out of town, leading the way. We then motored through
the Alazani Valley towards the arid and angular Azeri mountains, their craggy
multi-coloured sides resembling the geometric patterns of ancient Eastern rugs.

I only remember snippets of the journey (I was only two), but my older
brother Sasha recalls playing chess with Bakunian boys in the courtyard and on
large balconies where Armenians and Azerbaijanis sat together drinking strong
tea spiked with wild thyme, leisurely tossing dice over ornate backgammon boards.

We decided to visit the Caspian Sea, seven of us rammed into our Zhiguli,
stopping on the way by the roadside. My parents don't believe me, but I clearly
remember a huge clay tandyr oven, its incandescent mouth filled with golden
molars. An industrious vendor kept sticking more of these huge oval teeth
inside the oven's mouth. It turned out to be the freshest bread we had ever
experienced. We ordered one, the size of a massive oblong platter (or at least
it seemed enormous to us children). By the time the second bread was passed to
Uncle Styopa through the car window, the first bread had disappeared at the back.

We kept driving on towards the vast inland sea, the removable tinted screen
covering the rear window doing nothing to protect us from the blistering sun.
All I remember is the oil derricks; monstrous metal storks bobbing their heads
up and down, and terracotta hills forming a striking geometric backdrop.

We finally reached the beach. It was so wide and so endless that it afforded
my 28-year-old mum the opportunity to have her first driving lesson. Women at
the wheel were still a rarity at the time – in fact, I remember my mum dropping
me off at my music school six years later and little boys from my class giggling
and pointing at mum's tiny Fiat Uno saying, "A woman at the wheel, tee hee!" I
still recall the mixture of pride and embarrassment that I felt at that moment.
"My mum's so cool, why are they giggling?" Confusion.

Georgian wine, Georgian soul

Georgian wine, Georgian soul

I don't think I knew about wine, or what I loved about wine, until I tried Georgian wine. The recently fashionable "natural wine" movement, just like fermentation or the promotion of organic produce, is actually as old as the Caucasus mountains. Georgians claim to have invented winemaking, and I believe them. Wine flows through Georgians' blood; it is in their DNA. And not even the Soviets could completely beat it out of them, as the traditional, non-intensive methods of winemaking are now enjoying a huge, and very welcome, comeback.

My trip around Georgia in October 2015 was completely unplanned. I posted a message on social media saying that I would be recreating a 30-year-old journey I had made with my parents and brother but this time just with my brother Sasha, and people started writing to us. I believe in going with the flow, so rather than following a predetermined route, we travelled spontaneously.

After the first few days in the capital Tbilisi, we were told that a wine producer in Imereti, towards the west, was waiting for us to join him at a local wine festival. Once we had arrived, a red-bearded man sought us out from the crowd and handed me a glass of his orange-tinged wine. I had heard of orange wine as a trend, but had never understood what it was about. I tasted it, and the depth blew me away. Only later did I found out that he was one of the most revered Georgian winemakers, producing only 2,000 odd bottles a year (just him and his wife), and his wines were available in esteemed restaurants such as Nopi, Ottolenghi and Terroirs in Central London.

It was a heavy day and night; Georgians do not take drinking lightly. My brother was kidnapped by a group of men from a nearby village (they were impressed by his colourful toasts and rhetoric) who fed him copious amounts of sub-standard Khvanchkara red wine. By three in the afternoon he was lying on the grass, chicken pecking at his feet. I kept going. The next day, for the first time in my life after such an intense drinking session, I had absolutely no hangover.

Now, let me explain.

Winemaking plays an integral part in a lot of Georgian families, yet producing and bottling natural wine is still fairly rare. There are two different paths that formed the basis of the natural winemaking movement. Some families refused flat-out to use chemical sprays on their vines, having seen how the vines and the earth were weakened as a result, and always stuck to natural methods in their vineyards. Most people in the villages wouldn't even consider using industrial yeasts/sulphur/filters/other additives for their home drinking wine. Other people, disappointed with the wine available to drink in the shops, took to the villages, deciding they could do better, and by investigating among their elders what it was about the pre-Soviet wines they remembered and loved from their childhoods, turned to natural winemaking as the inevitable solution.

Slowly, in the early 2000s, winemakers began to meet each other through the Slow Food movement and Elkana, an organization devoted to organic agriculture in Georgia. Importers visited, and Georgian natural wines took off on the international scene. This is the real deal, naturally fermented grape juices that taste like honeysuckle, farmyards and dried apricots. They go so well with food, especially Georgian food, which is layered with strong, complex flavours.

These are not your easy-drinking bland aperitif wines, made on a terrifyingly industrial scale. These are not even your expensive commercially produced wines laden with sulphur. They are alive, like any fermented product should be. They live, and they change. The vines are encouraged to co-exist with their wild surroundings, the true terroir. Growing among wild summer savory, clover and a microcosm of insect life, the vines are allowed to do their thing, with only minimal guidance from their caretakers. In the cellar, these wines are not manipulated. They are truly just from grapes. And when you take into consideration a list of up to 70 non-grape-based additives that are allowed even in organic wine, that constitutes a huge difference in not just the quality of what you're drinking but also what you're putting into your body. I have never personally had a physical hangover from drinking these wines. If you choose to put natural food into your body, why destroy that positive impact with a beverage on steroids? Then again, if you shun this natural wine ode and decide to drink the rubbish from your corner shop, turn to the chapter entitled Pain, Be Gone on page 162.

Silk & black snow

Soviet Union, 1950s. The mountaintops of the Nagorno-Karabakh area in the heart of Azerbaijan were still peppered by both Armenian and Azerbaijani villages, some of each yet to be completely wiped out by war between the two communities 35 years later.

In autumn, rows of grape vines interspersed with the crimson of pomegranate orchards weaved the way to the village of Godrud, the peaks covered in heavy snow. But it was in June when Nina, the eldest of the many children in their extended family, would leave the capital Baku to spend the following three months with her grandparents in the predominantly Armenian Karabakh mountains.

Before they set off, their car would always be filled with:
• a sack of flour
• a sack of sugar
• a sack of wheat, to feed the chickens
• a sack of rice, which was incredibly important
• 3 large jars of clarified butter, prepared in advance by her grandmother
• a large canister of sunflower oil
When they arrived at the village, Nina's grandfather would always buy (and then sell again if anything was left at the end of their stay) the following:
a white horse, to swiftly move around the hills
chickens, cockerels and turkeys
a few sheep, rams and goats

I switch on my dictaphone and listen to this again and again. This recording has sparked a desire in me to visit the Caucasus. I am desperate to find Nina's demolished house in Karabakh, but the war broke out there again very recently and I don't dare to risk it.

The dictaphone is on again, and Nina's soft voice continues:

"From the end of May to the end of the summer, we would be sent to Karabakh. Our parents never worried about us, as a whole lot of us children would spend time with our grandparents in the small mountain village, including our second and third cousins.

"I was the oldest of all the children and I had to look after the little ones and entertain them, so I had my hands full. But it was fairly easy, as it was the safest of places.

"Our life in the mountains was full of adventures. We would all leave in the morning and disappear until lunchtime, but nobody would even begin to worry. People were everywhere, and we knew everyone very well.

"We used to play in the mountains and pick bunches of wild flowers. There were a lot of walnut trees around the village, which were taboo. For some obscure reason, walnut trees were considered harmful if grown near humans or in orchards, so they were only found just outside the village.

"Even though it was strictly forbidden, we used to climb up the trees to pick the young, green walnuts with the creamiest soft flesh. I was the best tree climber, so would climb right to the top and pick loads of the green walnuts. Afterwards, we would go to the mountain spring to wash our hands of the brown residue you get when you mess around with green walnut shells. Grandmother would always check if our hands were brown when we came home, so the mountain spring saved us from more than one rebuke.

"We also used to fetch water from the mountain spring to drink, and for my grandmother to make her beautiful fermented pickles.

"My grandfather was a unique human being. He fell in love with a particular mountaintop and decided to plant an orchard there, right on the peak. Only the best-behaved child had the honour of washing grandfather's feet after work. And this was how we were brought up – to have the utmost respect for the elderly. Nowadays, if I ever tell my eight-year-old granddaughter off, she looks at me blankly and says, 'Ninochka, this is ridiculous.' Yet my grandfather never once in his life raised his voice. He was the calmest and wisest man I have ever known. He only had to look at us with a slightly painted expression and the mere fear of his disappointment would make us behave immediately.

"It was generally a very friendly environment and I remember the Azerbaijanis and Karabakh Armenians living happily side by side. Then all of a sudden things changed, and hatred was ignited. To me it seemed to come out of nowhere; I speak Azer, Armenian, Ukrainian and Russian.

"My grandmother would pick wild herbs in mountains to make a dye. We were taught to weave by the Azerbaijani women and we all made a rug together, so each little piece in this rug has been made by one of the many girls and women in my extended family. This is our pure wool relic of the summer of 1964.

"Our picnics were the best. Of course, the occasion was more than a picnic; it was a ritual. A donkey would be loaded with provisions and some woven rugs, and we would set off to the most spellbinding spots. A little kid (goat, not child) would be taken with us to be slaughtered right there and then (don't faint, it was part of our culture) and cooked slowly over wood embers.

There was also a swing on a tree just by a huge crevice. When the swing would go forwards, it took your breath away, as there was nothing but an emerald abyss below. Yes I know, climbing walnut trees was forbidden, but swinging over the edge of a mountain was OK!

"We also made silk. There were a lot of mulberry trees that never produced fruit but they had enormous leaves. Men would pick the dry branches and put them in a room, which was kept at a certain temperature (rusty thermometers hung all over the room). They would then implant about 7g [a generous ⅛ oz] of silkworm eggs and wait. Soon enough the room would fill with crunchy munching sounds. The silkworms would work their way through a ridiculous amount of dried leaves daily, leaving only the branches behind. The mulberry branches were then replenished every day until the silkworms started moving their heads from side to side, which indicated that they were ready to build their cocoons. Each cocoon would have a hundred-metre-long thread, and every person, including the children, would set out to untangle each cocoon. For two days the cocoons would be swiftly collected, untangled and sorted into prime product (to be taken in hessian sacs on donkey back to factories, where the cocoons would be steamed to kill the silkworms inside) and rejects. We would steam the rejects ourselves to make silk threads so that everybody would have a small beautiful silk trophy left over from all the hard work.

"Before the war [1988-1994] there were a number of Azerbaijani villages and towns in Karabakh, and incredible vineyards and pomegranate orchards, but everything was destroyed during the war. Karabakh is now connected to Armenia by a corridor, and travel between the two countries is strictly forbidden."

The power of intention, thought, nature & cooking

Cooking for me has always been a little bit more than putting a few ingredients into a pot. I grew up with women who listened to the particular bubble of a pot. My grandmother used to say (this is a literal translation): "When the stew gets enough spirit in it, it's time to put the dumplings in." The word *dukh*, which means "spirit" and is related to *dusha*, meaning "soul", has always been part of my food-making, but it's been very casual – something I never analysed, just did.

When we arrived in Lankaran, an Azerbaijani city near the southern border with Iran, we were immediately told that a special dish was being prepared for us by three women and that they had started making it at five in the morning. We were to be taken there and help them finish cooking it. It was already 12 noon.

So from five in the morning, three women in their late 60s or 70s had been stirring something in a huge cauldron suspended over a roaring fire. You may think Macbeth, but it was a much more positive affair. The reason why I mention the women's ages is because while they were engaged in those eight hours of continuous stirring, they were ageless, as fit and full of spirit as any 20-year-old I met that week. They were making *samani khalvazi* or wheat halva. Traditionally lots of wheat berries would be left to sprout, and as soon as the white sprouts appeared, they were cooked in a pot over fire. Kilos of sugar would be added and the pot continuously stirred for eight hours. There are now only a handful of women in each village who have the knowledge and skill to make this dish.

Wheat is of course a sacred symbol of birth and abundance. So *samani khalvazi* is not a dish that is cooked casually. It is only ever made if there is a serious intention, an active wish to be made, such as wishing to get pregnant or wishing for someone to get better. As you stir, you think about your intention, and with every rotation of the oar-like wooden spoon, you will come closer to its materialization. I loved this labour-intensive but meditative way of cooking; it's these meditative qualities of cooking that have made me fall more deeply in love with it. At first it was a necessity – try dicing 5kg (11lb) of chillies in a restaurant kitchen and not fall into a trance. It would be torture, and really boring. But allow yourself to lose your mundane thoughts and dream instead, and your containers are filled with perfectly diced chillies within an hour, and perhaps you have also untangled something in your heart and mind. Repetition of a single action is both mesmerizing and therapeutic, and making hundreds of those tiny *dyushbara* dumplings (see page 111) are the representation of my sanctuary, my expression of love.

Another colourful tradition in Azerbaijan is the making of *fisinjan* – a chicken and pomegranate dish that in some parts of the country is most desirable when it becomes black. How do they make it black? They throw a horseshoe into the pot with the stew to oxidize it! Not only do they do that, but also shout at the tops of their voices something along the lines of: "I wish the neighbour's daughter falls in love and runs away with a man!" Forget Tinder, get your Auntie to make you *fisinjan* Azerbaijan-style. And if no suitor appears, at least both of you would have had a side-stitching laugh and a delicious lunch.

Ingredients

Caucasian food, at least in the ex-Soviet Union region, has always had a reputation for being meat-heavy. However, while Russian *shashlyki* or Georgian *mtsvadi* or Azerbaijani *shish* kebabs are commonly served in restaurants, in the modest everyday lives of most people in the Caucasus, especially in rural areas, meat is considered a treat – as it should be. Sheep as well as other animals are well-reared in small numbers, and the meat is of superb quality. My grandparents in the south of Ukraine managed to rear their own animals despite the stratospheric rise of Soviet industrialization, enjoying meat only on occasion and making use of every part of the slaughtered beast without any waste.

When I had finished writing this book, I surprised myself at the size of the vegetarian chapter – it was the longest. I tried balancing it out with more meat recipes but then decided that, if vegetables, pulses, bread and dairy are the heroes of everyday eating, I shouldn't force the meat chapter to be bigger. And to be honest, vegetable dishes are the ones that I personally find the most interesting. It's all about the hits of flavour that such simple fresh ingredients can deliver when put to unexpected use. Pound mint, salt and green chilli together, for instance, and use to season mozzarella or lamb chops or stir through new potatoes or roasted vegetables. Or make some *matsoni* (homemade yogurt; see page 29) and serve with tender runner beans.

People in the Caucasus are still so connected to their local land and its produce, and more often than not these ingredients are beyond excellent – you can taste the love and care that went into growing them. And foraging for them is not a trendy buzzword – harvesting nature's gifts is still a way of life, and what a rewarding way it is.

The following are some ingredients that may throw you, but if you want to experience the authentic flavours of the Caucasus, I strongly recommend sourcing them and I have listed as many suppliers as I could find to help you (see pages 234–5). A jar of blue fenugreek, some dried marigold petals and *adjika* salt will last you ages. But if you can't find some of these exotic ingredients, it's not the end of the world; *Adjapsandali* (see page 41), for example, will remain incredible even if it doesn't see any blue fenugreek. This is a food-lovers' book, so all you really need is good-quality produce – great vegetables, small amounts of excellent meat, a few spices and some raw creamy milk if you would like to have a go at making fresh cheese (see page 107). Don't let the constraints of a written recipe hold you back – buy some fresh vegetables from your farmers' market, be creative with substitutions and open your mind to new techniques. Cooking should not be a robotic act: instinct, intuition and constant tasting and adjusting the flavour balance are essential skills that will help you become an outstanding cook, just like the Caucasians. They use traditional recipes, sure, but they are also some of the most creative cooks I have ever come across. How can you fail to be with ingredients so outstanding?

Spices

BLUE FENUGREEK

Utskho-suneli, as Georgians call blue fenugreek so sonorously, or *Trigonella caerulea*, as botanists term it a little more brashly, is said to be endemic to Georgia, even though *utskho-suneli* means "foreign spice". In its dried ground form, it is one of the components of the Georgian *khmeli-suneli* spice mix (see below), so if you can't find it on its own, source the spice mix online and you will get a taste of that funky Georgian flavour into your dishes. Some say that the smell and taste reminds them of the standard fenugreek used in Indian cooking, albeit milder. I agree that it is subtle, but to me it has very little to do with the bitter fenugreek that we are more familiar with in the West, its flavour being more akin to the most complex yet gentle garam masala. When you experience good-quality blue fenugreek, try as you may to register that it's just one spice, it smells like a heady mixture of ten spices.

KHMELI-SUNELI

This is Georgia's famous spice mix, which varies in constitution and can contain up to 20 different dried herbs and spices. It usually features dried blue fenugreek leaves and seeds, coriander, fennel, cloves, marigold, mint, dill seeds and summer savory, but may also include dill, marjoram, hyssop, parsley, basil, bay, cassia bark and even a little hot chilli. You can use a little of this instead of blue fenugreek on its own (see above) or whenever red *adjika* salt is specified.

DRIED YELLOW MARIGOLD PETALS OR POWDER

Often called, to my ears rather sweetly, *kviteli kvevilli* or yellow flower, dried marigold (*Calendula officinalis*) is also frequently referred to as Imereti saffron, which is perhaps why I sometimes struggle with it as a flavouring, because it seems to have the faintest of aromas and not to be contributing much. But used in Red Adjika Salt (see page 62), it adds a further earthiness, almost a mushroom-like umami if the accompanying spices are used in moderation. It's also valued for the colour it brings to dishes.

Flavoured salts & pastes

ADJIKA

The term *adjika* refers to a rather salty, aromatic chilli condiment not too dissimilar from Tunisian harissa or Syrian *muhammara*. It can be as liquid as ketchup or come in the form of dry chilli salt pellets. The best I have ever tried was from Samegrelo in western Georgia, but Abkhazia in the same region also prides itself on its own versions of this spicy flavour enhancer. In fact, it most probably originated from Abkhazia, as the name comes from Abkhazian word for "salt". It is the intensely flavoured dry variety that I bring back with me to the UK in kilos, which no one really makes at home but instead buy ready-made at the market. However, having seen how it's made, I wanted to re-create it myself (see page 62).

The ingredients normally include red chilli, garlic, blue fenugreek and salt, although sometimes it can be very mild and contain more red peppers than chillies. There are also varieties where green chillies or mint are included (see page 25). Walnuts can also feature in *Abkhazi adjika*, or tomatoes in watered-down commercially produced versions in Russian food stores, which I wouldn't waste my money on.

SVANETI SALT

This is famous in Georgia, and is made in a very similar way to the red *adjika* salt (see above) in Samegrelo. Besides salt, it contains raw garlic and a wide variety of spices including blue fenugreek and dill seeds.

Fruit and vegetables

ALYCHA PLUMS

Green, hard and extremely sour when unripe, these plums make an exceptional addition to herby spring lamb stews. They can be preserved whole, or turned into a dry paste or fruit leather (see page 228).

BARBERRIES

Luckily Yotam Ottolenghi has already done some groundwork in introducing this beautiful wild berry to a wider audience. Barberries are not only used extensively in Middle Eastern cooking but also in Georgian and Azerbaijani dishes. Sold as whole dried berries or sometimes in flakes, they bring a distinctive acidity to dishes, added to stews or stirred through fresh salads; as versatile as they are delicious. You can find dried barberries fairly easily in Middle Eastern shops and online, but if you ever get a chance to travel to Azerbaijan, Armenia or Georgia in the summer, visit The Deserters' Market in Georgia's capital Tbilisi and keep an eye out for fresh, plump, juicy barberries from the mountainous region of Tusheti.

CHICKPEAS

If you use chickpeas, dried are always best. However, if time is of the essence, do try and source chickpeas in brine, which are sold in glass jars at good Italian delis. I think they have a superior flavour and texture. I've learnt this trick from the cook and food writer Sabrina Ghayour, who really knows her chickpeas.

EKALA

From what I can gather, ekala is primarily an Imereti (a region in western Georgia) wild plant with the rather amusing botanical name of *Smelax excelsa*. It is a type of spinach, even though it's nothing like the iron-rich, leafy vegetable we are used to in the West. Being an ingredient junky, constantly on the lookout for new and exciting items, it immediately caught my eye at markets all over Georgia. It has spindly curly offshoots not unlike the tendrils of a grape vine. If you have ever tasted grape vine shoots, this has a similar, slightly sour flavour, but it's also a little musky and wild-tasting.

FRUIT LEATHER

Called *tklapi* in Georgia, *lavashak* in Armenian and *lavashana* in Azerbaijani, fruit leathers are rife in the Caucasus, just as they are in Iran. Huge 20-litre (4½-gallon) pots of fresh fruit juice or purée are balanced over some shimmering fruit wood logs, slowly bubbling and reducing into a thick syrup. Given the volume, it can take a day or two for it to reduce sufficiently. Then it is poured over a cotton sheet, spread into a thin layer and when dry kept between sheets of paper all winter. Pieces of it are then given to kids as delicious natural treats. Sometimes these sour–fragrant sheets are soaked in water and then added to stews and soups to add a gorgeous fruity note. You can find them ready-made, but you can also (if you have a glut of superb fruit) follow my recipe and make your own *tklapi* (see page 216). And here you are not restricted to specific ingredients; just use the best local fruit available.

JONJOLI

Colchis bladdernut is the unglamorous common name for jonjoli, which sounds like wind chime crystals singing in the wind, whereas bladdernut sounds... Let's forget about bladdernut. Jonjoli looks as beautiful as its Georgian name – a tall shrub with grape-like clusters of unopened white flower buds. Georgians pick them and pack them with salt into humongous jars, then leave them to ferment. No caper, which it is often likened to in flavour, comes even close in comparison. By way of a substitute, look for so-called acacia trees in your area, actually false acacia or black locust (*Robinia pseudoacacia*), as their unopened flowers, which appear in late spring, are sometimes used instead of jonjoli in Georgia (be careful not to use any leaves, as they are toxic). I have served jonjoli many times in London and beyond, and people go crazy for it. What is this strange, dangly, caper-like bud they ask? Jonjoli! Sorry, I can't stop saying it – jonjolijonjolijonjoli...

PURSLANE

The wonderful sea purslane is to be found in the UK growing wild in wetlands by the sea. But in Georgia and other regions of the Caucasus (as well as Greece, Cyprus, Turkey and other Mediterranean regions) it grows where no other plant will, pushing its meaty, salty, slightly tart leaves through gravel on the side of the road, popping up in people's neglected gardens, anywhere. It can be eaten raw, but I like to blanch it for just 20 seconds to mellow its flavour and make it more digestible. I am lucky enough to live on the porch of London's Turkish and Cypriot heaven that is Green Lanes in North London, and my local greengrocer sells it in the summer. If there is no way you can get hold of it, don't despair. You can substitute sea purslane or use some other beautiful greens such as Swiss chard or spring greens – their earthy tones will work equally well.

SORREL

Ahhh, sorrel. It is my favourite leaf. I grew up with it in Ukraine and I encountered it again in the Caucasus. But common sorrel or garden sorrel (*Rumex acetosa*) is also native to the British Isles and to be found throughout Europe and in parts of North America, yet it's an often forgotten or at least underrated leaf. I really hope that we can all start a sorrel revolution and make it widely available. It is so easy to grow, tastes like a lemony dream and is beautiful added to broths or used fresh in salads.

TKEMALI

Alycha plums, either in their green unripe state or ripe yellow and red, are used to make one of the most important condiments in Georgia, *tkemali* sauce (see page 23 for a recipe). I don't know if Caucasian cooking could continue if *tkemali* suddenly disappeared; it's almost sacred. Some cook it for a while, resulting in a thick, spicy, garlicky purée, but it's the fresher, barely cooked version that I love the most. This sauce is served with everything – grilled meat, shallow-fried river trout, cooked vegetables. Beetroot cooked in *tkemali* was for me a revelation bordering on an epiphany – beetroot and plums – but of course! Earthy, firm and sweet beetroot paired with slightly caustic and juicy plums; a Burton and Taylor marriage in its intensity (see page 13 for a recipe).

UNREFINED SUNFLOWER OIL

I mentioned this beautiful ingredient in my debut book *Mamushka* and I feel I have to mention it again, as Georgians, like their Ukrainian sisters and brothers, adore this oil. Nothing to do with the highly processed sunflower oil we are used to in the West, it is deep golden in colour and nutty in flavour. Imagine toasting a load of sunflower seeds and then squashing them over your salad – this is what it will taste like. And it is used (raw, never cooked) extensively – over salads, over fermented vegetables, always over jonjoli (see left) and thinly sliced red onions. It is also served with a light sprinkling of chilli flakes and sea salt for bread to be dipped into, just like Italians do with superb olive oils.

WET GARLIC

This is simply new-season, young garlic (i.e. wet behind the ears, if it had some) and luckily it is becoming more and more widely available with each spring.

WILD GARLIC

The people of Armenia, Georgia, Azerbaijan and other Caucasian countries love wild herbs and they collect and cook with hundreds of different varieties, which makes you realize how urbanized and removed from nature the rest of us are. But we don't have to be. Even if you live in a city, you can pick wild garlic easily. For example, in the London area, come spring you can hit Walthamstow Marshes – just Tweet the wonderful food writer Rosie Birkett who lives locally and she will direct you to the best spots.

Herbs

OMBALO

Imagine marjoram and mint making love on some swampy marshes and bearing a wild herb child as a result. This is what ombalo (*Mentha pulegium*, also commonly known as pennyroyal) tastes like to me. It sings and makes your head spin when you taste it in a sauce or sprinkled over some incredible tomatoes. If you can't source it, spearmint mixed with marjoram is closest in flavour, but if that is also difficult to find fresh, use a little bit of good-quality dried mint in your sauce.

PURPLE BASIL

Azerbaijanis call this *reikhan*, a suitably regal-sounding word. It is a rather flamboyant king of herbs in my opinion. Sweet, with a slight aniseed kick, he is far superior to his green brother. Laid out among other herbs on the table as part of a standard feast accompaniment to other dishes (just pick a sprig and eat it all, including the stalk) or sprinkled into a saffron-hued *dyushbara* broth (see page 111), it adds a curious layer to most dishes. It also loves the company of other soft herbs – chop it up and mix with a little tarragon and mint, lots of coriander and a handful of dill, then add to your butter-roasted chicken at the end of cooking. The flavour will blow your socks off. It grows surprisingly well in my garden in the summer, but do check out the vegetable and herb suppliers on page 234 if you would like a bunch sent to you instead.

SUMMER SAVORY

In Eastern Mediterranean and in Georgia, a few wild plants of the mint family are known by the same name, so it took me some time to figure out what it was that Georgians called *kondari*. Is it oregano, wild mint, wild thyme or mountain savory? It turns out that wild winter savory (*Satureja montana*) and summer savory (*Satureja hortensis*) are the plants that Georgians call kondari and are used extensively in cooking. A Middle Eastern name for it seems to be *za'atar*, although this is also the name given to Syrian oregano (*Origanum syriacum*) as well the *za'atar* spice mix, just to add to the confusion! Summer savory has a more pronounced flavour than winter savory, and this is the one they use most.

Wild things

In the mountains of Georgia you can forage for and eat wild sorrel leaves, bilberry leaves and berries and wild strawberries and raspberries, which taste about five times more intense and sweet than the cultivated varieties. Wild walnuts are smaller but again more pronounced in flavour. How can all of these ingredients not be, as they grow alongside each other, drinking mountain spring water and influencing each other's flavours? Some plants I've encountered in Svaneti, a gorgeous northwestern province of Georgia, I have never seen anywhere else – the thorny kotzakhuri shrub with edible leaves, letsiri stalks, barberry leaves. Imereti mushrooms were the best I have ever eaten in my whole life, and I've sampled some spectacular mushrooms. If you ever get the chance to drive from Tbilisi in the direction of western Georgia and it has been raining, shout and stop the car if you spot roadside vendors. They are foragers and they might have something that Georgians call *mchadi* mushroom (*mchadi* being a local dense corn flatbread). The mushrooms are small, very dark in colour and very dense. Even when cooked, they retain an almost raw-like, crisp texture. The flavour is... almost indescribable. The closest

I came in comparison was sucking the juices out of a red Spanish prawn's head, so imagine that but in a mushroom context.

Dairy

BUTTER

I tried buffalo butter in Azerbaijani Qebele region that made me want to stuff it in my pocket and eat it like cheese later in the car. I've encountered a similar product in Georgia, homemade by many a woman in the mountains. Butter can be much more than what we are used to. One of the reasons why milk and all the things that come from it, such as cheese and butter, are so incredibly good in the Caucasus is because of where the cows, buffaloes, goats and sheep roam and what they eat. Seeing cows dexterously picking rosehips with their lips, as well as a thousand other wild-growing plants, puts it all into perspective. Even though I have not encountered buffalo butter in the UK, I know a person who makes the most incredible cultured Jersey butter. Young Grant Harrington (he is literally in his early 20s!) is currently making some of the most spectacular fermented butter in the country. Of course, you can use any good-quality commercial butter.

CHEESE

They make spectacular cheese in the Caucasus. So special, so flavoursome, so widely available but sadly not so in the West. I despaired writing some of these recipes. How on earth can they translate to another context if the cheese doesn't taste of wild meadows consumed by tiny agile Caucasian cows? There is, however, a way forward. If you don't get to travel to Georgia or Armenia and sample the real thing, check out your local farms and small-scale producers for artisanal, unpasteurized cheeses (see also the list of suppliers on page 234 for guidance). They may not be made using the same techniques, and they will no doubt be made from the milk of massive dairy cows rather than tiny Georgian cows, but it is absolutely possible to find the right stuff. If you care about your food and quality produce and the people who put a lot of time and effort into creating it, you will be able to come very close to replicating the flavours that knocked my socks off in dreamy Caucasia. If all else fails and you are a cheese-making enthusiast, check out the fresh cheese and *suluguni* recipes (see pages 107 and 108) and make your own!

MATSONI, MAZOON & KATYK

These are basically homemade yogurts that use a Caspian strain of bacteria to make a starter called *deda* in Georgian, which translates as "mother". Once you've made this kind of yogurt at home, you won't be able to look at supermarket yogurt in the same way again, as the flavour and texture differ significantly from what we are used to commercially, and it is full of healthy bacteria. You will need to find proper milk, by which I mean raw milk. Some say that it's OK to use non-homogenized milk, but I think raw is actually what is needed here. You may also need to source some yogurt bacteria. Check the supplier list on page 234 for all these items.

MILK

In the ancient western Georgian Samegrelo dialect (some say language), *bzha* means "milk", but it also means "sun", which must make it the most gorgeous homonym in linguistic history. "Darling, pour some sun into my tea, would you?" I wish English was as effortlessly poetic sometimes. But it makes sense. This is how holy dairy products are considered to be, not only Georgia but in the whole of the Caucasus. Picture small agile cows, the size of a large goat, hopping around the mountains, munching on rosehips, berries, flowers and a cornucopia of wild herbs. They are so tiny and muscular that they produce half the volume of milk that a dairy cow provides. But just imagine the unique flavour of that milk – it is very nutritious and fatty, and tastes of the wild mountainous terrain.

Meat

KURDYUK FAT

This is fat from the rump of a special fat-rumped (or fat-tailed) breed of sheep found in Azerbaijan and Central Asia that look like they have massive humps on their bums. This fat is DELICIOUS. It's firm in texture and doesn't melt away but crisps up when cooked. In Central Asia they have a ceremonial dish where they cook the whole rump with the fat intact until super crispy and then slice and eat it. A Thai friend of mine who has tried it now dreams of having it with some spicy *nahm jim* sauce, which I can relate to. I doubt if you will be able to find *kurdyuk* fat anywhere in the West. Some Turkish halal butcher's may have something similar, but unfortunately it may never be as flavoursome as what you would find in the Caucasus and Central Asia. So go to your butcher and ask him to give you trimmings from the best-fed, tastiest lamb they have, such as salt-marsh lamb – it will add an incredible flavour. We have learnt to use pig's fat in the Ukraine in a similar way, for instance when we make manty, or pork dumplings – we use good pork and mix it with a little lightly cured pork fat that we call salo. Good Italian *lardo* (in chunks rather than thinly sliced) will also do the trick.

Wine

Here I am talking exclusively about the Georgian natural wine revolution. The ancient winemaking traditions of Georgia with its hundreds of endemic grape varieties had been quashed by the industrialist behemoth that was the Soviet Union. Land was seized, only commercially viable grape varieties planted and thousand-year-old techniques abandoned. Giant Georgian clay fermentation pots called *qvervi* and the masters that made them almost disappeared. And then, circa 2006, a miracle happened. The near-vanished art was rediscovered by prominent French winemakers and then picked up by the descendants of traditional Georgian winemakers all over the country. And they starting making wine, the real deal, using pre-industrialized, naturally fermented grape juices that taste like honeysuckle, farmyard and dried apricots. These are not easy-drinking wines that you would sup in a bar. These are wines that really shine when paired with delicious foods, even with foods that are generally considered hard to match with wine.

Part of the reason for this is because many of the red wines are made using a white-grape method, involving very little skin contact (maceration time) and resulting in light-bodied fresh reds. And white wine grapes are allowed to ferment along with their stalks and skins, like reds normally would be, and left together for nine months in the *qvevri* (or, as Georgians say, left with their *deda* or mother), the natural "womb" hand-crafted from local slate and clay, buried into the Earth's belly, producing the most spectacular orange wines known to humanity.

These wines are a far cry from the bland aperitif wines made on a terrifyingly industrial scale. They are not even comparable to expensive commercially produced wines laden with sulphur. They are alive like any fermented produce should be; they live and they change. The old grape vines are allowed to grow naturally in their wild surroundings, the true "terroir", among wild summer savory and clover, with minimum human intervention. As the doyenne of wine writing Alice Feiring observed, "... how a thinking person could actually believe agriculture was irrelevant to flavour... people who were committed to organic produce forgot that grapes that made wine were produce as well... It was commonplace to eat organic yet drink conventional." And I agree with her. If these thoughts resonate with you, or if you are simply curious, I highly recommend her book *For the Love of Wine*.

To discover some of my most favourite wines and producers, see page 234. Since some of them have made it on to the wine lists of Yotam Ottolenghi's restaurants, they definitely deserve a place on your wine rack at home. And besides, I have personally never had a hangover from drinking them; slow brain, sure, but not that throbbing physical pain. But if instead you decide to shun this natural wine ode and drink the rubbish from your corner shop, turn to page 144 and the chapter entitled Pain, Be Gone for some effective remedies!

Suppliers

SPICES & CONDIMENTS

The suppliers below stock spices such as *khmelisuneli*, blue fenugreek, fruit leathers and other unusual ingredients.

Caucasian Spice Box
www.caucasians.co.uk
For fenugreek, *tkemali*, jonjoli etc

Cornish Sea Salt
www.cornishseasalt.co.uk

Steenberg's
www.steenbergs.co.uk
Good, natural salt for brines and ferments

English Saffron
www.englishsaffron.co.uk

Belazu
www.belazu.co.uk

Persepolis
www.foratasteofpersia.co.uk

Seasoned Pioneers
www.seasonedpioneers.com

Hambleden Herbs
www.hambledenherbs.com

The Spice Shop
www.thespiceshop.co.uk

Georgian Gourmet (US)
www.georgiangourmet.com

World Spice Merchants (US)
www.worldspice.com

VEGETABLES

Good-quality produce as well as some unusual herbs like purple basil, wild garlic and sorrel can be found below.

Vadasz Deli
www.vadaszdeli.co.uk
Fermented vegetables

Wild Harvest Ltd
www.wildharvestuk.com
Foraged wild foods and spices

Organic Delivery Company
www.organicdeliverycompany.co.uk

Natoora
www.natoora.co.uk

Riverford Farm
www.riverford.co.uk

MEAT

It is important to use very good-quality meat, and to eat it not too often. The best quality beef and pork can be found here:

Piper's Farm
www.pipersfarm.com
Some of the finest ethical meat you can buy delivered to your door

Evers Field Organic
www.eversfieldorganic.co.uk
Great organic meat, door-to-door

Capestone
www.capestone.co.uk
Free-range poussin and chicken

Turner & George
www.turnerandgeorge.co.uk

DAIRY
Neal's Yard
www.nealsyarddairy.co.uk

Greyscheeses
www.greyscheesedirect.co.uk

Hook & Son
www.hookandson.co.uk
Raw milk

Emma's Dairy
www.gazegillorganics.co.uk
Raw milk

Moorlands Cheesemakers
www.cheesemaking.co.uk
Rennet

Ampersand
www.butterculture.bigcartel.com
Hand-crafted cultured butter

Natural Georgian Wine
www.lescaves.co.uk

GUEST HOUSES IN GEORGIA
Fangani Family Guest House
Vealge Becho (near Mazeri)
Svaneti, Georgia
Tel: +995 598 42 61 92
Email: inu.fangani@gmail.com

Guest House Ketino Sujashvili
Qvemo Gergeti Str.22,
4700 Kazbegi, Georgia
Tel: +995 571 03 24 39
Email: ketinosujashvili@mail.ru

Marina Nariashvili
Guest House Edemi
Rustaveli Street 105a
Akhaltsikhe, Georgia
Tel: +995 599 18 51 59
Email: 105edemi@gmail.com

RESTAURANTS IN GEORGIA
Azarphesha
2, Pavle Ingorokva St,
Tbilisi, Georgia
Tel : +995 322 98 23 46
E-mail: info@azarphesha.com

Poliphonia
23, Amaghleba St,
Tbilisi, Georgia
Tel : +995 557 63 71 43

Vino Underground
15, Galaktion Tabidze St,
Tbilisi, Georgia
www.vinounderground.ge

Pheasant's Tears
18, Baratashvili St.
Sighnaghi, Georgia
www.pheasantstears.com

Barbarestan
D. Aghmashenebeli Ave.
132, Tbilisi 0112, Georgia
Tel: +995 322 94 37 79

Culinarium
1 Mikheil Lermontovi St,
Tbilisi, Georgia
Tel : +995 32 2 43 01 03
Email: info@culinarium.ge

Khasheria
23, Abano St,
Tbilisi, Georgia
Tel: +995 322 72 11 57

Café Littera
13 Ivane Machabeli St,
Tbilisi 0105, Georgia
Tel: +995 595 03 11 12

Index

Bold pagination indicates main recipe

Author's acknowledgements

So many kind people have been involved in making this book possible - if I fail to mention someone, please forgive me. And, reader, forgive the soppiness that follows, I cannot help it.

Thank you Octopus, the best cookbook publisher in the world, and to Stephanie Jackson, who has given me this opportunity and more. Thank you for letting me keep my voice and my vision, I know how lucky I am – not a lot of authors get this.

Sybella, you are the most skilled editor I have ever met. When I read the edited text, it is hard to pinpoint what you have done, but I know you have done something, giving my ramblings such a smooth flow. Thank you for your gentle patience and encouragement.

Thank you to Denise Bates, Caroline Brown, Kevin Hawkins and everyone at Octopus who has helped make *Mamushka* such an immense success.

Miranda Harvey and Juliette Norsworthy – thank you for creating such a timeless, laconic design, and for including so much of my writing without it looking overbearing.

Grace, once again, thank you for transferring my vision into the cover – it's another classic.

Cara O'Sullivan, thank you for your beautiful hand-cut art of a map – it is now hanging, framed in my kitchen. You are an amazing talent.

Thank you, Tabitha Hawkins, for such an amazing job with the props.

Thank you Ariella and Aoife for being the coolest, sweetest agents one can hope for. I am so chuffed I have not let you down.

Thank you Elena Heatherwick for giving our project so much more than was ever expected. For sacrificing time with your son and for giving it your all. As my brother Sasha said, "Elena photographs souls". You really do – souls of people, souls of landscapes and your food photography is unique and timeless. This book is also yours, it would not be the same without you. I love you, you are my kindred spirit.

I would like to thank my Aunt Nina Grebenyuk, half-Armenian, half-Ukrainian, who inspired me with her stories of her childhood in Karabakh. Hours of our conversations have now travelled from the dictaphone on to these pages, giving them so much depth, colour and meaning.

A special thank you goes to Keti and Zezva Maghlakelidze of Caucasian Spice Box, who were the first link in the spontaneous chain of people who have followed and selflessly helped me research the area in the most natural way possible. Keti, thank you for all your help, you define Caucasian hospitality without me ever having visited your house!

Thank you also to Nino Baratashvili, you have inspired the "*dedakatsi*" essay and beyond. Also your mum and grandmother's recipes are some of the most cherished – I want you to know that.

Thank you to John Wurderman and Ketivan Mindorashvili for all the stories, thoughts, feasts and for connecting me with the most incredible people. Gia and Tina Rokashvili, thank you for welcoming us at Pheasant's Tears and for sharing your time, knowledge and outstanding recipes. Who needs a Michelin star when one can eat food like yours, Gia?

So many precious recipes in this book would be missing had it not been for Ketino Sujashvili, Marina Nariashvili, Galina and family, Zhuzhuna and Anna, Tea Chitadze. Also my sweet adoptive Georgian mother Ia Kerzala – you are amazing – thank you for giving me your recipes and also a crash course on Somegrelo dialect and all things etymology.

The Fangani family: Tina, Lasha, Amiran – you are some of the kindest, warmest people I have ever met. I will never forget how you cared for us in your guesthouse with that medieval chapel hanging around socasually in your back garden! You live in one of the most beautiful places in the world.

Another special thanks to one of my now dearest friends, Enek Peterson, for your guidance; editing and contributing to my essay about wine; for your kindness; the amazing dishes you created when we were cooking together and for endless inspiration. You are the future, and an immense, natural talent – I hope the people in Georgia see it and you get to cook just the way you cook at Vino Underground.

Thank you to the Akobidze family for giving us your beautiful home in Tbilisi when you did not even know us during such a sad and difficult time for you all. I will never forget your kindness.

Thank you to all the natural wine makers, their wives and mothers for welcoming us and sharing the beautiful wines and recipes. I am so proud to know you, Nestan and Ramaz Nikoladze, and of course sweet Tsegunya with your immense energy.

Thank you for your time and inspiration Tamaz Dundua, Irakli Cholobargia, Anastasia Lundqvist, Tekuna Gachechiladze. Thank you to all the kids from Artana for providing sanctuary and keeping me sane when I thought I was on the brink of physical and mental exhaustion (my sweet friends Tengo, Ketino and Kakha Berishvili, Tamuna, Ramazik, Sandro – thank you).

Thank you to our guides Shota Lagazidze (I too love vegetables, especially in spring) and to Akaki for taking us all around Georgia and for deep conversations, light laughter and some excellent Georgian tunes.

Thank you Anya Von Bremzen for connecting me with Zulfiya and Rufat Kazimov, who are now like family to us. Zulya, I thought that Georgians could not be beaten in their hospitality, but you have matched them and more. Thank you for letting me meet your family in Lankaran, that was a truly special time. I will come back and bring the book for Mehriban, Nazilya, Shafak and Imran.

Farkhad Ashurbeyli and the gang, thank you for the incredible off-roading recipe hunt trips. I will never forget our adventures.

Thank you to all the brilliant recipe testers and friends: Caroline Parry (and also for your support as always), Sarah Eden, Sara Haider, Alissa Timoshkina, Mari Volkosh, Dara Sutin, Chris Bailey and John Holland, Sara Haider, Concepta Cassar, Thomas Eagle, Richard Snapes and Eve Hemingway, Nico Ghiraldo.

A special mention goes to Carl and Deb Legge (of Permaculture Kitchen) – thank you for developing all the cheese-making recipes, for explaining the science behind it and for testing them so expertly.

Allan Jenkins, thank you for giving me a kick when I needed one.

Thank you to all the amazing assistants: Brian Gamble, Harry Sergeant and others for supporting us and making things so much easier.

Diana Henry, thank you for your ongoing support – I want to be like you when I grow up.

Nigella Lawson, Jamie Oliver – thank you both, what an honour to have your words of support.

Alice Feiring, thank you for your books – your knowledge of Georgia and natural wines is inspirational.

To our mums Olga and Liliana for taking care of our small boys while we were away shooting for long periods of time. Single parenting is not easy, and we couldn't have done it without you. Tim Catley, thank you also for being such an amazing grandma to Sasha.

To my brother Aleksandr – please come back, we miss you painfully. And to my dad Petro, *dyakuyu tato* for all your hard work and for teaching me that kindness is the most important thing in the world.

Sasha, my son, I am sorry I am away so much, this is all for you, always. I hope you will be proud of your mum. Joe Woodhouse, thank you for finding me when I'd lost all hope, for changing my life, inspiring me and making me love. I now feel recharged and complete and utterly happy.